THOMAS HARDY'S
THE MAYOR OF CASTERBRIDGE

TRAGEDY OR SOCIAL HISTORY?

TEXT AND CONTEXT

Editors

ARNOLD KETTLE
Professor of Literature
Open University

and

A. K. THORLBY
Professor of Comparative Literature
University of Sussex

◆

BERNARD HARRISON
Henry Fielding's Tom Jones:
The Novelist as Moral Philosopher

JEREMY HAWTHORN
Virginia Woolf's Mrs. Dalloway:
A Study in Alienation

LAURENCE LERNER
Thomas Hardy's The Mayor of Casterbridge:
Tragedy or Social History?

Other Titles in Preparation

THOMAS HARDY'S
The Mayor of Casterbridge

TRAGEDY OR SOCIAL HISTORY?

Laurence Lerner

Professor of English at
The University of Sussex

SUSSEX UNIVERSITY PRESS

1975

Published for

SUSSEX UNIVERSITY PRESS

BY

Chatto & Windus Ltd
40 William IV Street
London WC2N 4DF

*

Clarke, Irwin & Co Ltd
Toronto

Hardback ISBN 0 85621 042 0

Paperback ISBN 0 85621 043 9

© Laurence Lerner

Printed in Great Britain by
Cox & Wyman Ltd
London, Fakenham and Reading

CONTENTS

INTRODUCTION

This essay is an attempt to answer the question, What is the experience of reading *The Mayor of Casterbridge* like? The question is not as simple as it looks: that must be the excuse for writing 100 pages on it, nearly a third of the length of the novel itself. I shall divide my answer into two parts. The first – which is much shorter – is an attempt to capture the immediacy of reading, to set down the impact which the book makes at the moment of putting it down: to answer, we might say, the question: What *is* the experience of reading *The Mayor of Casterbridge*? In one way, of course, this is the only question that matters. Like all works of literature, what *The Mayor* offers us is a structured emotional experience, depending on the telling of a story, the language in which it's told, the people who take part in it: a narrative world in which we lose ourselves. If the book didn't offer us *this*, then nothing but a detached, academic curiosity could lead us to ask further questions about it; most readers would not even consider asking these, for they would not finish the book in the first place. First things first: and the first thing about *The Mayor of Casterbridge* is that to read it is all-absorbing and emotionally rewarding.

But literary criticism cannot stop there. If we are not merely readers but also *students* of literature, if we are even thoughtful readers, we shall want to reflect on our reading experience. We shall want to compare one novel with another, for the better understanding of what each has to offer, and the comparison may well imply preferences. And perhaps we shall reflect on the experience of novel-reading as such, asking not only what a particular book has given us, but what fiction gives us. We can try, in other words, to indicate what reading *The Mayor* is *like*.

Answers to this question can be divided into two groups. There are those which insist that reading a work of literature is different from reading anything else, because of the uniqueness of art. Though novels and poems may be built out of the materials of ordinary living, what makes them works of art is

7

a transmutation by which a human being becomes that utterly different entity, a fictitious character; by which the raw material of human passion is turned into a different kind of emotion, shaped and removed from immediacy; by which even words cease to have the practical function of ordinary words. 'The end of the enjoyment of poetry,' wrote T. S. Eliot, 'is a pure contemplation from which all accidents of personal emotion have been removed.' Among poets, Paul Valéry most admired those who 'ont essayé de construire une poésie que jamais ne pût se réduire à l'expression d'une pensée, ni donc se traduire, sans périr, en d'autres termes.' These remarks, claiming that personal involvement and the categories of normal thought are radically transmuted, even destroyed, in poetry, emphasise the discontinuity between art and the rest of our experience. Such a view is of course more often applied to poetry than to the novel, and more often still to music (where it is more or less orthodox). Among novelists it is more likely to be used on Proust, say, or Virginia Woolf, than on Hardy and Zola; but any claim that the untranslatableness of aesthetic experience is the defining element in art must apply to any writer whose work is claimed as literature.

The other view, naturally, is that which stresses the resemblances between literature and other forms of discourse, which is happy to compare a novelist's account of a society with a historian's, or a sociologist's; which regards Hardy's novels as part of a life work that includes his essays, his letters, even his actions, using one to throw light on the others; which extracts opinions and philosophies from a novel, and is not unwilling to compare them with ordinary opinions and real philosophy; for which it is meaningful and important to ask whether Zola is a socialist in his novels, or Dostoyevsky a Christian, or Hardy an atheist. In this view, literature is often seen as a way of conveying values: the values of a particular philosophy, or a particular moral scheme, or a particular social class.

Let us call the first view purist, or aesthetic; the second it is harder to find a name for – impure, perhaps, or human, or continuous (meaning continuous with other forms of writing). I do not want to call it the moral view, for a reason that will emerge later. I ought now to range this essay with one or the other of these views; but before that a few preliminary remarks.

8

First, most great writers have held the second view. Traditionally, all those defences of literature that have assigned to it a moral purpose must count as 'impure'; perhaps also those which regard it as an imitation of life – and these are the oldest and most famous theories. Milton, writing his great poem 'to justify the ways of God to men', does not seem troubled by the fact that justifying is a perfectly normal non-artistic activity. George Eliot, insisting that she is an aesthetic not a doctrinal teacher, goes on to explain that she sees her function as 'the rousing of the nobler emotions, which make mankind desire the social right, not the prescribing of special measures', and we realise that the emotions she wishes to arouse are of the same kind as those that determine our actions in the real world. Not until the twentieth century, under the influence of theories of art that stress its uniqueness, is it easy to find writers willing to place themselves in the first camp, and even then there has been a lively resistance from writers who continued to stress that their writing is a full and characteristically human activity. It is not difficult to see why this has been so. In writing a great novel or poem, an author draws on the full range of his concerns as a man; and in describing what he has done, he is more likely to remember what he put into it than how he transmuted material that for him began as richly human.

Second, there is an obvious sense in which the first view is right and the second view is wrong. We would not even need the terms 'art' and 'literature' if there was not an identifiable activity which they describe, differing from any other activity. When we praise a poem or a novel, we necessarily find ourselves saying that it is not just a discussion but that in it the issues have somehow come to life; that the story does not merely satisfy our curiosity about life in rural Dorset, or among the washerwomen of Paris, but involves us in a somehow untranslatable experience; that it is not merely the poet's skill in handling metres or making points that moves us, but the magic of his language, the power that poetry alone possesses to take us out of our normal selves. Unless we find ourselves saying something like this we do not know what literature is, and we have no way of distinguishing *Paradise Lost* from Milton's treatise *On Christian Doctrine*, or *The Mayor of Casterbridge* from Rider Haggard's *Rural England*.

Third, the task which this essay has set itself will be done in altogether a different way, according to which view we take. If our approach is purist, we shall need to define as carefully as possible the nature of the aesthetic experience; we shall concentrate on the internal organisation of the novel, and the discussion will carefully exclude similar but ultimately irrelevant material, that does not form part of the novel as a work of art. Our interest in Hardy the man and in his ideas and his environment will be strictly subsidiary, for Casterbridge is not Dorchester. Whereas if we take the 'continuous' approach we shall constantly widen instead of narrowing our range of interest, we shall add and compare instead of excluding, we shall move from the book out into the world instead of always from the world into the book; for Casterbridge is very like Dorchester.

The very title of the series, *Text and Context*, perhaps reveals that our approach will be the second; but in taking the second approach, I shall try never to lose sight of the element of truth in the first. To say that a novel springs from its author's ideas is not the same as saying that it is the exposition of a philosophy; to say that a poem embodies his deepest emotional experiences is not to claim that its main interest is as a biographical document; and to remind ourselves that a writer was dealing with a real time and place should not lead us to reduce novels to the same kind of historical evidence as newspapers and wage schedules. Literature is part of a human world; but it is a unique element in that world.

I

TEXT

This is the first of Hardy's novels which he named after its main figure; and then, to reinforce the point, he added a subtitle, 'The Story of a Man of Character'. What he wants us to notice seems clear: that this is to be a book dominated by one man, and that the centre from which the action derives is that man's highly individual personality, his tendency to impose himself on the world (for that of course is what 'character' means here).

Title pages should be treated with respect, but not automatically accepted: they show what an author thought was important in his novel, which is probably, but not necessarily, what is important. When for instance Hardy added to the title page of *Tess of the D'Urbervilles* the sub-title 'A Pure Woman' he defiantly asserted that there is a morality of nature that excuses Tess's sexual fall in contrast to the social morality that condemns it. By doing so he certainly called our attention to one of the novel's central themes, but the very touch of defiance in his assertion suggests that he has not completely solved the question of how the two are related, and whether moral language is appropriate to Nature's law. But in the case of *The Mayor of Casterbridge* I believe the sub-title is a true guide, and corresponds to the experience of reading. By this I mean two things.

First, and most obviously, Henchard *is* a man of character. He is impulsive in his loves his hates and his decisions. It is completely credible that he should have made a fortune as a corn merchant and then, unbalanced by his jealousy of Farfrae, that he should have lost it. It is completely credible that he should have urged Farfrae to stay in Casterbridge and become his manager on the strength of one brief conversation, that he should have confided in him and pressed him into intimacy, and then that he should have turned against him with such bitter revulsion: this is not an uncommon pattern between the middle-aged employer and the young newcomer, and with a man like Henchard it seems more probable than ever, and takes a more intense form. Hardy knew that he had created a masterly character-study, and with pardonable pride he pointed it out: and it is right that a discussion of the novel should begin with this most obvious but still central point, the dominance of the masterly, convincing, central figure. There is almost no limit to the examples. The fight with Farfrae in Chapter XXXVIII, for instance, doubles and redoubles on itself as it unfolds in a way which is full of surprises yet completely plausible.

Henchard, who was once Farfrae's employer, is now working for him; and he has just suffered the public indignity of being shaken by the collar, like a tramp, when he pushed forward to greet the royal visitor with his home-made speech. Farfrae's action had been necessary and justified, but so far from cooling Henchard's indignation this (naturally enough) fans it further, as he projects on to the other his own uneasy sense that he has behaved foolishly. The fact that Farfrae had acted without malice, and is not likely to bear a grudge, makes things more unbearable still, for it is this very coolness and detachment that reminds Henchard how he has exposed himself emotionally by his impulsive acts of friendship and hatred: Farfrae's calm aggravates Henchard's insecurity.

Here then is the ground prepared for an act of murderous aggression, yet built into Henchard's nature is a rugged sense of justice, based wholly on intuition, that leads him to the grotesque action of binding his left arm to his side so that they can fight on equal terms. Because of the impulsiveness of his reflections Henchard is given no train of reasoning, simply the sudden thought that issues in his saying aloud (it had to be aloud) 'I'm stronger than he'. The major premise, that they ought to fight on equal terms, he does not even formulate to himself: what he notices is the discrepant fact that the terms aren't equal. That is what we mean by intuitive morality.

Hardy is writing with great narrative skill here: it is this remark that tells the reader what is going to happen – or almost tells him, and the very matter-of-fact description of Henchard tying his arm that then follows (the concentration on the details exactly paralleling Henchard's own consciousness) is accompanied by a dawning realisation on our part of what he is going to do. Such skill is not perhaps typical – Hardy's narratives are wonderfully conceived, but he is not greatly gifted in the small local techniques of controlling the reader's response; and it is certainly less important than the marvellous revelation of Henchard's character through his action. This continues through the whole chapter, culminating in the final reversal by which Farfrae is spared. The struggle is very even (Henchard had judged the difference in strength well) but finally:

> Farfrae's fair head was hanging over the window-sill, and his arms dangling down outside the wall.
>
> 'Now,' said Henchard between his gasps, 'this is the end of what you began this morning. Your life is in my hands.'
>
> 'Then take it, take it!' said Farfrae. 'Ye've wished to long enough!'

This is exactly the remark (though Farfrae was hardly aware of it) to save his life: for Henchard, now that his victory is complete, suffers a sudden reversal:

> Henchard looked down upon him in silence, and their eyes met. 'O Farfrae! – that's not true!' he said bitterly. 'God is my witness that no man ever loved another as I did thee at one time . . . And now – though I came here to kill 'ee, I cannot hurt thee! Go and give me in charge – do what you will – I care nothing for what comes of me!'

When two wolves are fighting and one admits defeat, he presents his neck to the other for the jugular vein to be bitten through; whereupon the victor turns his head aside, and allows the defeated wolf to rise. In this way, fights between two males do not weaken the species by killing off healthy adults. This built-in mechanism for the survival of the species, which is described in Konrad Lorenz's book *On Aggression*, seems to underly Henchard's action, though there is no reason to suppose that Hardy knew about it. To find the point made by a biologist is to find a theoretical basis for a feeling which the text conveys immediately; that Henchard is a man of intense and direct impulse. It is a kind of reassurance to find that there is a biological basis for behaviour that had seemed convincing and in character.

We can also explain the action in terms of Henchard's relationship with Farfrae, which is one of love–hate; and the former love, by asserting itself at the very moment when hate is victorious, shows us how inextricably the two are mixed. This is not, in fact, the only moment at which Henchard comes to the edge of taking revenge, and then draws back. Shortly before (in Chapter XXXIV) he had called on Farfrae in order to collect Lucetta's love letters, left behind in the safe of the house he had once lived in, and settled down to read them to the unsuspecting Farfrae, intending:

> to effect a grand catastrophe at the end of this drama by reading out the name; he had come to the house with no other thought. But sitting here in cold blood he could not do it. Such a wrecking of hearts appalled even him. His quality was such that he could have annihilated them both in the heat of action; but to accomplish the deed by oral poison was beyond the nerve of his enmity.

If he had known that Lucetta was listening outside the door, waiting in terror for the moment when he revealed her name, his delight in the trick he was playing would have been even greater – and so perhaps would have been his inability to carry it through. We have here a similar situation to that in the loft: uncontrollably eager for revenge, Henchard draws back at the last moment because the victim speaks to him in a way that shows him, suddenly, that he no longer wants to crush him.

Henchard is by far the most important person in the book; no one else can compare with him in prominence, and no one else is like him in temperament. All the others can be seen as foils to Henchard. Susan provides the extreme contrast. The only moment at which she shows spirit is in the very first chapter, when she announces that if Henchard touches the money, she will go with Newson. Her resistance here is a way of displaying Henchard to us: the brutality with which he has treated her is reflected in the way she is finally goaded into leaving, but only (the responsibility is wholly his) by at last seizing the opportunity he is thrusting on her in order to make his own complaint against the world. When she reappears in the story nineteen years later, she is wholly passive. Henchard takes the decision to remarry her, and Henchard's is the only voice that counts in the re-united family. It is an obvious device, this, to set this dominant, impulsive figure off by giving him so submissive a wife, and it allows Hardy to write one of his livelier scenes among the working-folk of Casterbridge, set off by Christopher Coney saying 'Daze me if ever I see a man wait so long before to take so little.'

We learn a little more about Elizabeth-Jane than about her mother, and she has a far more active role in Henchard's life, though Hardy never allows himself to get too interested in her. He tells us of her love of reading, but never names a single book she reads; he tells us she is good-looking, but in completely general terms; and when she is given a firm character-trait, such as her 'craving for correctness' ('Any suspicion of impropriety was to Elizabeth-Jane like a red rag to a bull') we feel she is somehow not given it for herself. It is useful for the plot that she should be like this, since Lucetta used her as a confidante, trying unsuccessfully to wring from her some approval of her marriage to Donald; and it is (as Hardy does not fail to point out) a trait we'd expect, after her early troubles with her mother. It is necessary for the balance of character that Elizabeth-Jane should be virtuous, ordinary and sensible, and this is what Hardy has made her.

He took even less interest in Newson, who is there almost entirely for contrast with Henchard. At first he seems an upright, kindly man, a good husband and father, whose disappearance resulted from consideration for Susan, when he realised she no longer felt able to live with him. Only after his reappearance at the end do we see him as light-hearted:

The door of the front room had been taken off its hinges to give more space, and . . . Henchard . . . could see fractional parts of the dancers whenever their gyrations brought them near the doorway, chiefly in the shape of the skirts of dresses and streaming curls of hair . . . By degrees Henchard became aware that the measure was trod by someone who out-Farfraed Farfrae in saltatory intenseness . . . He was sweeping grandly round, his head quivering and low down, his legs in the form of an X and his back towards the door. The next time he came round in the other direction, his white waistcoat preceding his face, and his toes preceding his white waistcoat. That happy face – Henchard's complete discomfiture lay in it. It was Newson's who had indeed come and supplanted him.

It is clear, surely, from this passage why Newson needs to be light-hearted: it enhances the gaiety of the marriage feast that jars so on the lonely man watching it, and makes it very credible that after Elizabeth-Jane's rebuke he should be too proud, and too bitter, to feel there is any further place for him in her life. Even Newson's last act – the decision to settle in lodgings in Budmouth so as to be in sight of the sea – takes on a fuller significance if contrasted with Henchard's very different decision to leave. Each of Elizabeth-Jane's fathers goes back in the direction he came from, one in casual nostalgia (and Hardy treats the lodgings in Budmouth with mild amusement), the other in fierce self-pity; one fades out of the story, the other dominates to the end.

Of all the persons in the novel, only Farfrae can compare with Henchard in interest, and even here it is difficult to think of him in isolation, so important is the contrast between the two. There are moments when Hardy is willing to pause and develop some aspect of Farfrae's nature without having Henchard immediately in mind – the first meeting with Lucetta, for instance, when we watch – with some amusement – the hard-headed young merchant falling under the woman's spell, embarrassed at the discovery that he has no wish to leave, though business awaits him in the market outside:

'Maybe I'll get into my market-mind when I've been out a few minutes,' he murmured. 'But I don't know – I don't know.'

Here Hardy is allowing himself a little simple comedy over the earnest young Scot falling in love, and we have forgotten Henchard almost as completely as Farfrae has forgotten that he had called to see Elizabeth. But the interlude is brief: Hardy would not have written it merely to show Farfrae falling in love with any woman. The involvement with Lucetta leads directly into rivalry with Henchard.

With the partial exception of Farfrae, then, all the other figures exist as foils for Henchard: and this is the other significance of the sub-title, which is meant to tell us not only what Henchard is like, but also what the book is like. Our experience of reading is dominated by our awareness of him. No one else is allowed to grow into wholly independent life. Hardy had never before created anyone like Henchard, and he never did again – pride, passion, obstinacy, self-pity, impulsive generosity mingle to make him unique, and above all his enormous vitality gives him a power that informs every page. Because he is so striking a figure, the novel offers us a headlong, intense and also completely coherent experience. This is why some of Hardy's admirers have felt it to be his greatest book.

* * *

To ask of a novel, Who is it about, leads us to concentrate on the characters in it: this is one way of thinking about our reading, perhaps the most obvious. But we can also ask, What happens: that will lead us not to the characters but to the plot. We do not simply ask, What are the events, for that would lead to a mere retelling of the story, but, What sort of pattern do they make. A novel is a sequence of events, and the experience of reading it will depend, in part, on how one event is shown to follow another. There is a form of narrative in which we are told, meticulously, how the crucial episodes came about. As an extreme example of such form, we can take the novels of the German writer Theodor Fontane. In Fontane's most famous novel, *Effi Briest,* there are two crucial events, Effi's adultery and its discovery by her husband six years later. With nineteenth-century reticence Fontane does not give us a scene of actual adultery, but one in which Effi travels alone in a carriage with her lover Crampas, who covers her arm with passionate kisses: we realise later that this episode was crucial for her. The discovery comes about through Instettin, her husband, accidentally finding a bundle of old letters in Effi's drawer when she is away. These are the two pivotal scenes in the book's action; and it is remarkable how much space Fontane devotes to explaining how each came about. We are told the exact composition of the party which set off to spend a day in the country, the exact series of rearrangements that led to Effi and Crampas finding themselves alone in the carriage, how their carriage came to be separated from the others, how it came to be delayed – all quite trivial details in themselves, but relevant to the question of how Effi's affair developed, with the kind of relevance appropriate to law-courts. Similarly in the case of the second event, we are told how Effi's daughter fell and cut her forehead, why Effi herself was away at the time, how in looking for bandages the servants happened to upset some of her things, how this led to the accident of her husband discovering her letters. This is Fontane's characteristic technique: though the story may stretch over several years, only a small number of days are chosen for actual narration. We are then given a detailed account of every circumstance, however small, which led up to whatever the crucial action may be. The effect of this is to impress us with the overwhelming power of circumstances. Fontane is interested in character, and what Effi does is certainly the result of the sort of person she is; but at the same time we are meant to feel that this expression of her nature had to make itself felt through a thousand particulars that might well have been different. And inevitably this leads us to feel that it was circumstances that caused the outcome – not unusual, unlucky, exceptional circumstances but simply a series of ordinary events that accumulates and becomes a series of shaping influences. If Effie had not married Instettin; if Crampas had not come to live in the neighbourhood; if they had had different neighbours; and then if there had not been that particular series of rearrangings – if if if. Change one detail and you might change everything. The story of Effi's life, in the hands of such a narrator, becomes a seamless web, in which we see the ripples of interaction caused by the smallest and most every-day events.

The narrative impact of *The Mayor of Casterbridge* is (surely) the exact opposite of this. Its effect is not continuous but jerky. Each episode is given without any introduction, and we move rapidly from one to the next; there is no lack of colourful event in Henchard's life, and Hardy seems inexhaustibly fertile in thinking up new ones to tell us. Whereas Fontane is like a careful witness reconstructing a series of interacting details on a particular day, Hardy is like a raconteur, telling a series of lively anecdotes as he calls them to mind. Henchard's unsuccessful preparations for public entertainment when a holiday comes – lavish, impetuous and in the end wasted; Henchard's gamble on a bad harvest; his conduct when he goes bankrupt; Farfrae's offer to let him have his furniture – these episodes and many others are introduced with little or no preparation, they all tell us something about the protagonists, and as usual with a good raconteur we feel there are a lot more he might have told us.

It is clear that Hardy realised the episodic nature of his plot, and was embarrassed about it. When it began to be published he noted in his journal 'I fear it will not be so good as I meant, but after all, it is not improbabilities of incident but improbabilities of character that matter.'[1] In the *Life* by his second wife, which we now know to have been virtually an autobiography, there is a similar remark prompted by the publication in book form:

> It was a story which Hardy fancied he had damaged more recklessly as an artistic whole, in the interest of the newspaper in which it appeared serially, than perhaps any other of his novels, his aiming to get an incident into almost every week's part causing him in his own judgement to add events to the narrative somewhat too freely.[2]

Perhaps we need not take altogether seriously these disclaimers and suggestions that plots so thickly packed with event were not natural to him. There is a similar disclaimer over his early novel *Desperate Remedies,* whose ingenuity of plotting is almost unbelievable; but so much ingenuity and elaborate irony of plot runs through the short stories that we must surely believe it to be something Hardy fell into naturally.

The effect of the tightly packed narrative of *The Mayor* is surely to give more prominence to the character of Henchard. What we feel we are seeing is not the relentless force of small accumulating details, but a series of examples of how one man behaved. What binds the episodes together is what they all have in common – the fact that they show what kind of man Henchard was. How can we fail, as we read the book, to see him as a man who makes his own destiny? Over and over to show us what he was like we are given examples of what he did; and the apparent assumption is inevitably that he did that because of what he was like. In that way it is a novel of character.

Of course, Henchard does not altogether make his own destiny: no one in Hardy's fiction ever does. A good deal of bad luck follows him, and at times there seems to be a perversity in things that treats him with something like malice. For example, when he finally decides to tell Elizabeth-Jane that she is his daughter he goes to look among his wife's papers to find a document that he can show her in corroboration; and finds instead a letter that tells him she is not his daughter. If he had not told her that she was he would not have found out that she wasn't, and Hardy does not hesitate to point out this irony to us. The weather too is particularly hard on Henchard: it ruins his entertainment in Chapter XVI, while allowing Farfrae's to be a great success, and it ruins his gamble on bad weather when he buys corn recklessly (Chapter XXVI and XXVII) – though the weather does, as a final twist, turn out bad after all, when he has sold at a loss. Henchard, it seems, is disastrously unlucky.

We shall have to say a good deal on this point later: it involves the whole question of Hardy's philosophy, and it is necessary – and illuminating – to compare *The Mayor* with the rest of his fiction. What we must certainly admit now is that such perversity in events will undermine our confidence that Henchard is responsible for his own destiny. Yet even in the examples just given, Hardy's concern seems to be less in the cruel mischance itself than in Henchard's response. The violence of his withdrawal of affection from Elizabeth, the fitful bad temper that develops into settled dislike – these are the result of Henchard's own impetuous nature, and of little else. And it was not really the bad harvest that ruined Henchard: it was his own stop-go policy, the violent urge to compete with Farfrae and ruin him, the trust in the irrational that took him to the conjuror and led to his gamble, and then the premature loss of trust in his own wild decision. In both these cases we can, after all, lay the responsibility on Henchard himself. The discovery of Elizabeth-Jane's parentage, the fickle weather, are ironic accident: what Henchard did in consequence is character.

And perhaps we should add that the malicious irony of things, even when not played down, undermines our belief in the autonomy of character less than Fontane's relentless particularising. Somehow the very arbitrariness of a Fate that strikes maliciously from the outside makes it less convincing as a cause than the power of everyday and interlocking detail: occasional blows, however terrible, do not hold us so tight as steady pressure. It may be too that we don't really believe in Fate as we believe in circumstances, so that the undermining of autonomy by Hardy rings less ineluctably true than the matter-of-factness of Fontane – or, to take an English example, George Eliot. Determinism, not Fate, is the true enemy of our belief in freewill.

* * *

Character and plot: there is one other element that is central to the experience of reading a novel – language. The most immediate impact any book makes is through the actual words used, and words in a work of literature are not a mere transparent medium through which we see the subject matter, and which have no effect in themselves. There is, unfortunately, less to say about the style of *The Mayor* than about any other Hardy novel; for Hardy seems to have taken some pains to write pellucidly, and the highly individual fingerprint that makes the language of *The Return of the Native* or *Tess of the d'Urbervilles* eccentric, clumsy, grotesque and deeply moving by turns, is here reduced to something much less obtrusive (though the clumsiness is not always absent). To try and capture and describe the flavour of the prose of *The Mayor,* it is best to quote a paragraph:

> Casterbridge, as has been hinted, was a place deposited in the block upon a corn-field. There was no suburb in the modern sense, or transitional inter-mixture of town and down. It stood, with regard to the wide fertile land adjoining, clean-cut and distinct, like a chessboard on a green table-cloth. The farmer's boy could sit under his barley-mow and pitch a stone into the office-window of the town-clerk; reapers at work among the sheaves nodded to acquaintances standing on the pavement corner; the red-robed judge, when he condemned a sheep-stealer, pronounced sentence to the tune of Baa, that floated in at the window from the remainder of the flock browsing hard by; and at executions the waiting crowd stood in a meadow immediately before the drop, out of which the cows had been temporarily driven to give the spectators room.

This is not a paragraph chosen at random, for the point it is making is central to the book – the dependence of Casterbridge on the surrounding countryside, represented here by the immediacy of physical contact. A social point is translated into a visual point, and since it is an oddity of juxtaposition we are being told of, the language mimes the oddity with touches of quaint wit. The bluntness of the contrast encourages a bluntness of language: 'deposited in the block' suggests that the making of a town was something immediate and artificial, quite different from how a corn-field grows, and so reinforces the contrast; and the quaintness is underlined by the reapers nodding to acquaintances as if they are momentarily absorbed into the urban world so close to them, the world where people stand on pavement corners, as if to emphasise the idleness that contrasts them with the reapers. And to support all this Hardy uses a purely linguistic effect, one that is endemic to English, and always available to the sensitive stylist: the contrast between Latinate vocabulary (the words longer, more abstract, more sophisticated, more concerned with niceties of behaviour or appearance) and the blunt immediacy of the Saxon. The contrast between the farmer's boy and the town-clerk behind his office-window is emphasised by the monosyllabic directness of 'pitch a stone'; even more striking is the contrast between the official terminology of the judge pronouncing sentence and the not-even-Saxon immediacy of Baa.

Hardy clearly enjoyed himself writing this passage; its very quaintness seems appropriate to the subject, and its language is able to mimic part of what it says.

At that point we must stop: to say more would be to discuss the nature of Casterbridge, and the significance of the theme of town and country, for the rest of the novel, for the rest of Hardy, for the age he was writing in. Over and over, this account of the immediate experience of reading *The Mayor* has beckoned us outside that immediacy, and invited us to explore its implications. It is time to follow these beckonings: to move from text to context.

THE LITERARY CONTEXT

The first context must be that of other novels; for the most obvious way to ask what anything is like is to compare it with what is similar. And so my first comparison is with Zola.

Emile Zola, born in 1840, was Hardy's exact contemporary, and the novelist to whom he was most frequently likened by contemporaries. Hardy's reviewers never tired of accusing him (it was usually an accusation) of introducing French naturalism into England. When *Tess of the d'Urbervilles* was published, the *Review of Reviews* wrote:

> the influence of so-called 'realism' as understood in France in the latter part of the nineteenth century, is strong both for good and ill in Mr. Hardy's latest work, which in some respects is Zola-esque to a degree likely to alienate not a few well-meaning persons.[1]

When *Jude the Obscure* was published, *The World* wrote that:

> Mr. Hardy seems to have become equally enamoured of the methods of Zola and Tolstoi – Zola of *La terre,* and Tolstoi the decadent sociologist.[2]

If then, we want to see more clearly what *The Mayor of Casterbridge* is like by comparing it with another novel, by another novelist, what better than *La terre,* Zola's long passionate novel about the countryside. The vast agricultural plain of La Beauce, stretching northward from the Loire, with Chartres as its capital, provides a setting very like Wessex: a world of its own in which generations have pursued what seems an unchanging pattern of exploitation of the land. *The Mayor* appeared in 1886, *La terre* in 1887: a comparison can hardly fail to tell us something interesting.

Since both novelists are writing about (and constantly mention) Nature, we should begin by saying that their world is always a world of men. Even at their most lyrical (and in their different ways both can be lyrical) they never see Nature as a mystical presence, but always as the basis for economic activity: the earth is the provider of food, and the setting for the life-cycle of man and beast. Hardy wrote in his journal in 1876:

> An object or mark raised or made by man on a scene is worth ten times any such formed by unconscious Nature. Hence clouds, mists, and mountains are unimportant beside the wear on a threshold, or the print of a hand.[3]

The fact that *The Mayor* is set in a town does not diminish the author's concern with the land, but helps to give it this man-centred and practical outlook. Casterbridge, as we are several times vividly told, was intimately related to the surrounding countryside; it was 'the pole, focus or nerve-knot of the surrounding country life', and the fact that it 'lived by agriculture at one remove further from the fountainhead than the adjoining villages' gives us a constant view of the land as where men work, as a centre of economic activity that is organised from Casterbridge. When Susan and her daughter first arrive in Casterbridge they walk past the shop-windows, and a very matter-of-fact paragraph makes this point clearly:

> The agricultural and pastoral character of the people upon whom the town depended for its existence was shown by the class of objects displayed in the shop-windows. Scythes, reap-hooks, sheep-shears, bill-hooks, spades, mattocks, and hoes at the ironmonger's; bee-hives, butter-firkins, churns, milking stools and pails, hay-rakes, field-flagons, and seed-lips at the cooper's.

– and so on through all the other trades. Lists like this are not tedious; they are a series of sharp individual reminders of man's relationship to the earth, a relationship that is not contemplative but active, that is based not on sensibility only but on man's body.

This is true of Zola too, but how differently! From the very beginning of *La terre* we are in a more terrible world. Where-ever we look, we see lust and greed. The cruelty of the Fouan family to one another is almost incredible: greed, violent peasant greed, dominates everything. It appears in its full force in the early scene of the dividing up of the property. Old Fouan has grown too old to work his land, and has therefore decided to share it among his children. In the lawyer's office he tries, gropingly, to explain why it is necessary:

And there was something left unsaid, something that was revealed in the emotion choked back in his throat; the endless grief, the heavy grudge, the rending of his whole body at this separation from his land – land so hotly coveted before his own father's death, and then cultivated with such avid tenacity and extended inch by inch at the cost of the most degrading avarice.

In the almost grotesque scene which ensues, every detail of the transaction, every franc of the pension which the children will pay, is haggled over. We suspect already that Fouan is being as foolish as King Lear in giving away his lands, and he suffers a fate quite as terrible, moving from one child to another in search of a home where he will be treated a little less cruelly, cheated a little less. We know that Zola intended the parallel with Lear, and on one terrible night Fouan is shut out of doors in a storm, till he is forced to come crawling back. Yet though our hearts bleed for his sufferings, this is not because there is anything in the old man himself to attract us. The children are simply behaving like their father. Worst of all is Buteau, a brilliant study in the narrow egoism of the peasant. The main action of the book shows how the relationship between Buteau's wife Lis and her sister Françoise is poisoned by sex and avarice as introduced into the household by him. The fury with which he opposes Françoise' marriage because it will require him to give up her half of the property is totally unscrupulous and, at times, violent.

There is nothing like this in Hardy. He has selfish characters, but they are never governed by such pure acquisitiveness, such a rage for land and money. If there is an acquisitive character in *The Mayor* it is no doubt Farfrae, but he has nothing in common with the Fouan family. He is honest, restrained, meticulous in obeying the rules – a careful accumulator. The moment at which acquisitiveness appears as something like a passion with him is very revealing:

'I've done very well this year. O yes,' he went on with ingenuous enthusiasm. 'You see that man with the drab kerseymere coat? I bought largely of him in the autumn when wheat was down, and then afterwards when it rose a little I sold off all I had! It brought only a small profit to me; while the farmers kept theirs, expecting higher figures – yes, though the rats were gnawing the ricks hollow. Just when I sold the markets went lower, and I bought up the corn of those who had been holding back at less price than my first purchases. And then,' cried Farfrae impetuously, his face alight, 'I sold it a few weeks after, when it happened to go up again! And so, by contenting myself with small profits frequently repeated, I soon made five hundred pounds – yes!' – (bringing down his hand upon the table, and quite forgetting where he was) – 'while the others by keeping theirs in hand made nothing at all!' (Chapter XXIII.)

This is the greed of the trader, not of the peasant. The rules which the Fouan family have to obey are those of nature, against which there is no appeal, but they have no respect for human laws of property, except perhaps at those moments when they can invoke them to protect their own. But Farfrae speaks like a man who operates in a world of man-made rules. He knows that his success depends on his reputation, so he must be careful to obey them. Indeed, the very exhilaration he shows here can be said to temper the greed: his satisfaction comes as much from the exercise of his skill as from the acquisition itself, and therefore depends on the fact that he did not cheat.

As well as greed, there is sex: the other dominant passion of Zola's peasants, indistinguishable from their love of land. Over and over in his writing, Zola links farming with fertility, the earth with lust, animal reproduction with human. In the very first chapter, Françoise (then 14) brings a cow to be served by a neighbour's bull; Jean (who later marries her) watches with a kind of awe her complete familiarity with reproductive processes, and it is the beginning of his attraction to her. The novel is scattered with passages of wild erotic description of the earth ('cette terre, violemment desirée et possedée'), whose intensity and outspokenness make Hardy seem tamely Victorian. Of Buteau's love of the land, for instance, Zola writes 'son amour n'est que le rut du mâle grisé par la terre.'

26

Let us look at a sustained extract from *La terre*, in order to see the quality of Zola's sensibility as it actually issues in the language. I have chosen a passage from Chapter 6 which describes threshing. Buteau has picked up a flail and begun to thresh, but unable to work up a good rhythm by himself, he called his sister-in-law Françoise to help him. For two hours they have been beating in silence:

> Françoise's cheeks were now flushed, her wrists were swollen, and her whole body was burning; she seemed to give off a kind of fire-wave which quivered visibly in the air, she was breathing heavily through parted lips. Wisps of straw were clinging to the loose locks of her hair. And with each stroke, as she raised the flail, her right knee stretched out her skirt and her hips and breasts expanded, straining the cotton; the naked shape of her sturdily-built girl's body was roughly revealed in a single long contour. A button flew off her bodice. Buteau saw the rim of white flesh below the sunburn across her neck, a bulge of flesh which kept showing up at each swing of the arm in the powerful play of her shoulder-muscles. He seemed to grow excited more than ever at the sight; and the flails went on beating, the grain leaped and fell like hail under the panting tap-tap of the two threshers.

The passage is dominated by the rhythm of the work, which is also seen as a rhythm of sexual intercourse. The threshing is a bodily process into which the two are totally absorbed, and every detail of its physical effect on them is given us. The richly sensual description never looks up from the two people threshing, just as they never look up from their task. We know, when we read this passage, that Buteau has been desperately trying to seduce Françoise, if necessary to rape her; and if we have read the whole book we can see in it a vivid preparation for the revelation that comes at the end. The writing is powerful and unsubtle, its implications obvious; and they are made more obvious still in the next paragraph, when Jean arrives:

> He felt a rush of jealousy and stood watching as though he had surprised them together, mated in this fiery work, striking

one after the other in exact time and running with sweat, so overheated and disarranged that it looked more as if they were making love than threshing corn.

For a comparison with this, *The Mayor* is not the most suitable of Hardy's novels, since agricultural work does not appear in it directly; but if we turn to *The Woodlanders* we can find a very similar – and very different – description of work: Giles Winterborne making cider:

In the yard between Grace and the orchards there progressed a scene natural to the locality of this time of the year. An apple-mill and press had been erected on the spot, to which some men were bringing fruit from divers points in mawn-baskets, while others were grinding them, and others wringing down the pomace, whose sweet juice gushed forth into tubs and pails. The superintendent of these proceedings, to whom the other spoke as master, was a young yeoman of prepossessing manner and aspect, whose form she recognised in a moment. He had hung his coat to a nail of the outhouse wall, and wore his shirt-sleeves rolled up beyond his elbows, to keep them unstained while he rammed the pomace into the bags of horsehair. Fragments of apple-rind had alighted upon the brim of his hat – probably from the bursting of a bag – while brown pips of the same fruit were sticking among the down upon his fine round arms, and in his beard.

She realized in a moment how he had come there. Down in the heart of the apple-country nearly every farmer kept a cider-making apparatus and wring-house for his own use, building up the pomace in great straw 'cheeses,' as they were called; but here, on the margin of Pomona's plain, was a debatable land neither orchard nor sylvan exclusively, where the apple-produce was hardly sufficient to warrant each proprietor in keeping a mill of his own. This was the field of the travelling cider-maker. His press and mill were fixed to wheels instead of being set up in a cider-house; and with a couple of horses, buckets, tubs, strainers, and an assistant or two, he wandered from place to place, deriving very satisfactory returns for his trouble in such a prolific season as the present.

The back parts of the town were just now abounding with apple-gatherings. They stood in the yards in carts, baskets, and loose heaps; and the blue stagnant air of autumn which hung over everything was heavy with a sweet cidery smell. Cakes of pomace lay against the walls in the yellow sun, where they were drying to be used as fuel. Yet it was not the great make of the year as yet; before the standard crop came in there accumulated, in abundant times like this, a large superfluity of early apples, and windfalls from the trees of later harvest, which would not keep long. Thus in the baskets, and quivering in the hopper of the mill, she saw specimens of mixed dates, including the mellow countenances of streaked-jacks, codlins, costards, stubbards, ratheripes, and other well-known friends of her ravenous youth.

Once again, the worker is intensely absorbed in his work, his hair and beard filled with bits of apple, as Françoise' hair was filled with the chaff from threshing. But we are not so swept along: there is not the same relentless rhythm, the same single-minded concentration. Hardy pauses to explain why Winterborne is there, and to tell us about the economy of cider-making. He tells it with a touch of rather clumsy learning ('on the margin of Pomona's plain') and with a rather coy economic reference – 'deriving very satisfactory returns'. How ill at ease that seems, in comparison with the straightforward listing of the tools in the Casterbridge shops; but as the description gets under way Hardy seems to lose his embarrassment, and grows absorbed in the details, listing the kinds of apples without apologising for his technical interest – though a touch of coyness does, unfortunately, reappear in the reference to the friends of her ravenous youth.

What is most striking about the passage is how unsensuous it is. There is none of the physical intensity of Buteau and Françoise, no suggestion of fertility, no sexual associations. This is all the more striking when we consider the situation: that the woman watching Winterborne is Grace Melbury, with whom he is in love. Zola's identification of Nature with sex is wholly absent. Giles Winterborne, who has a touch of the god of autumn about him here, is Hardy's natural man, who understands trees as if possessed of secret knowledge; and in all his relationships with Grace he shows the delicacy and scrupulousness of a perfectly bred gentleman. Uncontrollable desire is not associated with Nature in Hardy, but with sophisticated urban men and women.

It is not only about sex that Hardy is fastidious. One chapter in *La terre* describes the grape harvest, and by comparison we can see even more clearly how refined is Hardy's account of the apple harvest:

> Rognes stank of grapes. Everyone swallowed so many that behind every hedge the women pulled up their petticoats and the men let down their trousers; pairs of lovers, their faces stained with juice, kissed each other full on the mouth among the vines. It was always rounded off with the men getting drunk and the girls getting pregnant.

Hardy described his novel *Under the Greenwood Tree* as a rural painting of the Dutch school. No doubt there are Dutch painters and Dutch painters, some of them fastidious; but it is Zola whose writing is like a transcription of Breughel's landscapes, crowded with work, eating, drinking and fornication.

If Hardy lacks the violent sensuality of Zola, is he in compensation more capable of subtlety? To find a subtle treatment of sexual overtones we need to turn from *The Woodlanders* to *Tess*, the novel in which he begins (though in a complex and even confused fashion) to associate lawless sex with Nature. After Tess has given birth to her illegitimate baby, she goes to work in the fields, her younger sister bringing her the child to nurse during the dinner hour. During the morning we see her at work binding sheaves:

> From the sheaf last finished she draws a handful of ears, patting their tips with her left palm to bring them even. Then stooping low she moves forward, gathering the corn with both hands against her knees, and pushing her left gloved hand under the bundle to meet the right on the other side, holding the corn in an embrace like that of a lover. She brings the ends of the bond together, and kneels on the sheaf while she ties it, beating back her skirts now and then lifted by the breeze. A bit of her naked arm is visible between the buff

leather of the gauntlet and the sleeve of her gown; and as the day wears on its feminine smoothness becomes scarified by the stubble, and bleeds. (Chapter XIV.)

There is still nothing of the crude power of Zola to this, but it does, surely, show a sensitive awareness of the life of the body, and anticipates the later paragraph in which she suckles the infant. There is the simile of her holding the corn in an embrace like that of a lover – unpretentious, carefully observed, and stating the sexual theme. There is the matter-of-fact detail of her skirt, vividly rendered by the verb 'beating back'. There is (this time) an intense concentration on the task in hand which the prose captures, as in 'patting their tips with her left palm to bring them even.' And then there is an awareness of the way work bruises the body in the last sentence that is, surely, subtler than Zola, in the way the alliterative uncouthness of 'scarified by the stubble' gives place to the blunt fact of the last two monosyllabic words.

One other point of comparison between the novelists is too important to omit: that is their awareness of the modern world offstage, and how its concerns impinge on Wessex or la Beauce. In *La terre* they impinge far more: most of the issues being debated in the contemporary France find their way into the rural community, and even find their representatives there. Jésus-Christ, eldest son of old Fouan, sees himself as the man of '89, republican and democrat, and in a way he is, though it is a way that verges on parody. Canon, the Communist, preaches revolution and the dictatorship of the proletariat. Lequeu the schoolmaster announces the influx of cheap wheat from America and the terrible effect it will have on the rural economy. There are only two schoolteachers in Hardy, the utterly unintellectual Fancy Day in *Under the Greenwood Tree*, and Phillotson in *Jude the Obscure*, the novel in which Hardy finally left the rural setting – and even Phillotson has not got anything like this degree of political understanding.

The most striking invasion of the rural community by the outside in Hardy is the visit of the Royal Personage, and how completely free of issues it is. It sets off no ideological or class conflicts in Casterbridge, but a purely personal conflict, arising out of Henchard's unwillingness to accept that he has been displaced. His disruption of the visit is in no sense a protest against royalty nor even against the power structure of Casterbridge, it simply concerns his own position. If we compare two urban outsiders who buy their way into rural society, Hourdequin in *La terre* and Alec d'Urberville (or Alec Stoke, as his real name was), we find that Zola's character holds political views, is eager to experiment in farming, and becomes Mayor, in contrast to the purely pleasure-loving Alec, who brings nothing with him except his good looks and his unscrupulousness.

Hardy, we see, is a provincial. There is a much higher mental wall round Wessex than round la Beauce. And when it comes to rendering for us the customs of the community, we can notice that Zola describes the drawing of lots for conscription, a recent custom that country shares with town, whereas Hardy describes what is old and specifically rural (consulting the conjuror, or the skimmity ride).

In the end, this comparison is probably more use for the differences it has shown than for the resemblances, as is so often the case when we place two writers together in order to show the nature of each. We can understand why Hardy was irritated by the comparison, and claimed that he had drawn his realism from Fielding. Whatever contemporary critics may have said, Hardy was not a naturalist of the school of Zola. He does not stress the resemblances between man and beast, flaunt the scientific spirit in which he claims to study man, or trace everywhere the inescapable laws of a Nature that knows nothing of moral meanings. Only in *Tess* does he begin to toy with the idea that there is a law of Nature that contrasts with the moral law, and should be preferred to it (this can be seen, for instance, in the question whether Angel or Alec is Tess's 'true' husband) but even this is confused, for to call Tess a pure woman is to see Nature as moral after all. It was of course mainly – though not exclusively – *Tess* and *Jude* which provoked the comparison with Zola, but even here we are not really in the world of naturalism.

Hardy, fastidious and confused, provincial and quirky, contrasts strongly enough with the brilliant rhetoric, the eloquent intensity of Zola's aggressive naturalism. Each has much to offer that the other cannot give us, and we can only feel sorry for those contemporary reviewers whose haste to say that Hardy was offering something 'very French' seems to have led them to miss the very individual flavour of his novels.

* * *

And nearer home? The most illuminating comparison among English novels is with something much less famous. *Amaryllis at the Fair* is also as it happens exactly contemporary with *The Mayor*: it was published in 1886, and is by Richard Jefferies, who never achieved, nor (to be honest) deserved the enormous fame of Zola and Hardy. A prolific writer on rural subjects, and a not very successful novelist, he had a sensitivity that perceived the same things as Hardy, and those who know his work have often made the comparison. They offer us the same world.

It is astonishing that so bad a novel as *Amaryllis at the Fair* should be such a sensitive, impressive and fascinating book. Its badness consists of a total lack of plot, and the fact that what began as a promising study of how a young girl develops under the influence of a colourful dominating father and a self-pitying and depressive mother, suddenly ends in a description of her effete cousin and a purely static account of how they fall in love. The novel breaks off, as if Jefferies had decided that his concern was not to tell a story, but to set against each other a number of character sketches. So when we ask how character reveals itself in its response to events, and how this determines other events we realise that Jefferies has not even begun the necessary constructing on which a novel is built. However similar in sensibility and insight, even in talent, he may be to Hardy, he totally lacks Hardy's professional competence.

By far the most memorable of the character-sketches that make up the book is Iden, Amaryllis' father, and it is in this that Jefferies shows his real genius. Iden is a countryman who wants only to work in his garden, to gossip, to eat. He lives in a vivid awareness of the body and bodily processes. Here for instance is Iden planting potatoes:

The way in which he was planting potatoes was wonderful, every potato was placed at exactly the right distance apart, and a hole made for it in a general trench; before it was set it was looked at and turned over, and the thumb rubbed against it to be sure that it was sound, and when finally put in, a little mould was delicately adjusted round to keep it in its right position till the whole row was buried. He carried the potatoes in his coat pocket – those, that is, for the row – and took them out one by one; had he been planting his own children he could not have been more careful. (Chapter I.)

Iden is an almost grotesque figure – the previous paragraph describes his ragged coat, faded, threadbare and filthy. But he is never comic, because of the intensity of living that is felt in all he does. His concentration on meals is absurd – yet strangely impressive:

At all meals the rule was that there must be no talking, but at dinner the law was so strict that even to ask for anything, as a piece of bread, or to say so much as 'Give me the salt, please,' was a deadly sin. There must be absolute silence while the master ate. (Chapter II.)

That last sentence should not mislead us. Iden's authority in his own family is shaky, and bitterly resented by his wife. He does not impose silence in order to preserve authority, as would be the case in a family that accepted traditional hierarchy; he uses what authority he has to impose silence, which he requires for the sake of his reverential concentration on the sensuous pleasure of eating:

First he ate a piece of the dark brown mutton, this was immediately followed by a portion of floury potato, next by a portion of swede tops, and then, lest a too savoury taste should remain in the mouth, he took a fragment of bread, as it were to sweeten and cleanse his teeth. Finally came a draught of strong ale, and after a brief moment the same ingredients were mixed in the same order as before. His dinner was thus eaten in a certain order, and with a kind of rhythm, duly exciting each particular flavour like a rhythm, in its proper position, and duly putting it out with its correct successor. (Chapter III.)

It is not only eating that Iden concentrates on with such respect; the same passion is seen when he composes himself for his after-dinner nap:

By and by, his cheese being finished, he dropped his newspaper, and arranged himself for slumber. His left elbow he carefully fitted to the remnant of the broken woodwork of the chair. The silk handkerchief, red and yellow, he gathered into a loose pad in his left hand for his cheek and temple to rest on. His face was thus supported by his hand and arm, while the side of his head touched and rested against the wainscot of the wall. (Chapter III.)

Iden is not a successful man. Though a born countryman, his interests are too fitful and too erratic for a farmer. He is hopelessly in debt, and there is no prospect of his being able to pay his creditors; but this does not fill him with a sense of urgency. Nothing will break the rhythms of what he feels drawn to; and the obstinate strengths of the countryman are not flexible enough to adopt to the pressures that come upon him. He will plant what he wants to plant, not what is needed.

Iden and Henchard are both very similar and very different. There is even a certain resemblance in the family situation – a wife and one affectionate daughter; though Iden's wife, far from being a nonentity, like Susan, is a bitter and melancholic woman, whose criticisms of her husband reach the point of shrewishness:

'Sleep, sleep, sleep!' she cried, giving him a thump at each word. 'You've slept two hours. (Thump.) You sleep till you stupefy yourself (thump), and then you go and dig. What's the use of digging? (Thump.) Why don't you make some money? (Chapter V.)

Again, we are on the verge of the comic, as Jefferies clearly realises; and he has not quite the talent to avoid it and preserve the violence of the situation. ('Thump' is effective, but in the end rhetorically unwise.) With Amaryllis we are given an exquisite study of the impulsiveness of adolescence. She is a more attractive figure than Elizabeth-Jane, and her author is more interested in her. In both books, the womenfolk act as a foil that we may more clearly apprehend the character of the man.

What links Iden and Henchard, above all, is their obstinacy – the deep, passionate countryman's obstinacy that can pull them up to greatness or down to ruin. Iden has quarrelled with his father, and Amaryllis is the only link between them. The old man's money is urgently needed by Iden, but neither man will approach the other; and a rebuke to Amaryllis from her grandfather has the unexpected effect of winning her father's approbation for her, and causing a temporary reconciliation between her parents. It is an elaborate study in how pride punishes itself.

Henchard's obstinacy leads him, when Farfrae starts to show interest in his daughter, to recoil from the idea: what might have been an opportunity to heal the growing breach between the two men is, because of that breach, violently rejected by Henchard. But it was that same obstinacy that enabled him, in his revulsion against the sale of his wife, to take and to keep the oath not to touch liquor for twenty-one years; and this no doubt was a necessary condition of his success in Casterbridge. The qualities that for Iden are pure weakness in terms of worldly success are partly a help to Henchard, for the career of corn-factor is less rigid than that of farmer. But the temperamental similarity is very striking.

Jefferies and Hardy are the two most notable examples in late nineteenth-century England of the countryman as writer. The purpose that unites them is their resistance to the rural stereotype. 'Hodge', the popular name for the agricultural labourer, is to them a label whose purpose is to reduce individual human beings to a dummy, and they both insist that to get to know the countryman is to cease to see him as a stereotype. Jefferies makes the point in *Hodge and his Masters*, a series of sketches of rural life that is full of points of resemblance to Hardy's fiction: it sees the countryside from the farmer's point of view, and only at the end of his short life did Jefferies (who was by then becoming more radical) present the labourers too with sympathy. Hardy makes the point in his essay 'The Dorsetshire Labourer' in which he imagines a 'thoughtful person' who believes in the conventional Hodge spending six months living in Dorset, at the end of which:

Hodge, the dull, unvarying, joyless one, has ceased to exist for him. He has become disintegrated into a number of dissimilar fellow-creatures, men of many minds, infinite in difference.

36

Yet if we recall that the main characters in Hardy's novels (at least until *Tess* and *Jude*) are usually the social superiors of the chorus of rustics, who are seen vividly yet still, largely, as figures of comedy, we can wonder if Hardy too is in some way on the side of the farmers.

THE PHILOSOPHICAL CONTEXT

To compare Hardy with other novelists is to place him in an obvious context: but our curiosity need not stop there. For how are we to interpret the very fact of writing such novels? What is the meaning of our activity when we read them, and in particular when we read *The Mayor*? What sort of novels did Hardy write? The answer to this question will determine the wider context in which we find it helpful to see him.

There have been two main tendencies among Hardy criticism, which we may call the universal and the particular, or the cosmic and the social. In the one, the novels are seen as making statements about Man's place in Nature, about human destiny and human limitation, about the place of the individual life in a hostile or indifferent world – questions of the highest possible level of generality, timeless and unchanging issues. In the second, they are seen as emerging from a particular time and place, the product of historical conditioning – the south-west of England at a time of considerable social and economic change, the Dorset in which Hardy grew up and which he knew so intimately.

The contrast between these two tendencies is so marked, and so important, that I shall use it to give a structure to the rest of this essay. I propose first to talk about Hardy's philosophy of life, and about his novels as statements of man's tragic situation; this will lead into a discussion of *The Mayor* as tragedy, and Henchard as a timeless figure. Then I shall discuss Hardy's relation to the rural England and the society that produced him. The contrast between these two approaches involves not only two ways of seeing Hardy, it can imply two contrasting conceptions of literature.

It is clear that there are universal elements in *The Mayor*. The most obvious is the death of Susan Henchard, which is received by the townsfolk of Casterbridge, gathered at the town-pump, with a tragi-comic conversation that has become justly famous as a communal folk-reflection on death. Mrs Cuxsom describes the care with which Mrs Henchard had made everything ready for her funeral, including 'four ounce-pennies, the heaviest I could find, a-tied up in bits of linen, for weights – two for my right eye and two for my left.' She had asked them to bury the pennies afterwards, but:

> that man, Christopher Coney, went and dug 'em up, and spent 'em at the Three Mariners. 'Faith,' he said, 'why should death rob life o' fourpence? Death's not of such good report that we should respect 'en to that extent,' says he.

This earthy lack of reverence, that somehow implies a feeling for the permanence of living, could come from (say) the sub-plot of *Henry IV*: it is the earthiness of Falstaff's warm-hearted egoism. Yet Hardy is not just Shakespeareanising: he has not allowed the literary influence, real as it is, to overlay observation, and Christopher Coney's aphorism is both memorable and real, both Shakespearean and in real Wessex speech.

The last speech of Mrs Cuxsom, too, is a pure elegy on the matter of factness of death – any death at any time:

> 'Well, poor soul; she's helpless to hinder that or anything now,' answered Mother Cuxsom. 'And all her shining keys will be took from her, and her cupboards opened; and little things 'a didn't wish seen, anybody will see; and her wishes and ways will all be as nothing.'

The same thought is found in Hardy's poem 'Friends Beyond', in which he imagines the characters of his early novel *Under the Greenwood Tree* speaking to him from the grave; and Lady Susan says:

> You may have my rich brocades, my laces; take each
>   household key;
> Ransack coffer, desk, bureau;
> Quiz the few poor treasures hid there, con the letters kept
>   by me. . . .

A similar effect comes at the death of Lucetta. Henchard is watching outside the Farfraes' house at dawn:

> He saw the door gently opened, and a servant raise her hand to the knocker, to untie the piece of cloth which had muffled it. He went across, the sparrows in his way scarcely flying up

from the road-litter, so little did they believe in human aggression at so early a time.

'Why do you take off that?' said Henchard.

She turned in some surprise at his presence, and did not answer for an instant or two. Recognizing him, she said, 'Because they may knock as loud as they will; she will never hear it any more.'

Not quite so explicitly universalised this time – though the sparrows are clearly there to make us step back from the particulars of the story and see the death as an event in Nature. And not so eloquent either – Hardy seems to manage better in Mother Cuxsom's salty voice than in that of this anonymous servant. But clearly a deliberate echo of Susan's death.

Now if all the universalising in Hardy's fiction were of this kind, there would be little to say: to pause and show the resonance of a death will enrich a novel but need not change it much. Hardy held a philosophy of life more elaborate, more articulate and more pessimistic than that, and to think about his novels as statements on human destiny we must first of all look at this philosophy.

Hardy was a man of his time: he abandoned Christianity because he felt it to be no longer intellectually tenable, and we can see in his development reflections of the scepticism and pessimism of his age. He claimed that as a young man he 'had been among the earliest acclaimers of *The Origin of Species*,'[1] and when a Rev. A. B. Grosart wrote to ask his views on whether the horrors of human and animal life are compatible with the absolute goodness and non-limitation of God, he wrote in reply:

Mr. Hardy regrets that he is unable to suggest any hypothesis which would reconcile the existence of such evils as Dr. Grosart describes with the idea of omnipotent goodness. Perhaps Dr. Grosart might be helped to a provisional view of the universe by the recently published Life of Darwin, and the works of Herbert Spencer and other agnostics.[2]

The reading of Darwin destroyed several aspects of the traditional view of Nature. It was no longer possible to regard it as a book in which God's purpose could be read, since the mechanism of natural selection, postulated by Darwin, was characterised precisely by lack of purpose. If evolution had taken place by the effect of the struggle for survival choosing the fittest from innumerable chance variations, then it had taken place by accident: there was no design in Nature, and so there could be no argument from design to prove the existence of God. This was the effect of Darwin on many of the thoughtful men of the later nineteenth century, Hardy among them. It meant the poets' idea of Nature would have to change: it was no longer possible to see her as a moral teacher and spiritual guide, as Wordsworth had, or to claim 'Nature never did betray The heart that loved her.'

Hardy drew the conclusion that moral categories had nothing to do with Nature; that man was unimportant in a world fundamentally indifferent to him:

'If it be possible to compress into a sentence all that a man learns between 20 and 40, it is that all things merge in one another – good into evil, generosity into justice, religion into politics, the year into the ages, the world into the universe. With this in view the evolution of species seems but a minute and obvious process in the same movement.'[3]

That was written when he was 36; forty-four years later he spoke of 'Nature's indifference to the advance of her species along what we are accustomed to call civilised lines'.[4] The idea of man's unimportance when seen from a non-human perspective seems to be one Hardy always held: we find him in 1887 complaining that philosophers 'cannot get away from a prepossession that the world must somehow have been made to be a comfortable place for man.'[5] And his attitude to Christianity was, in consequence, an odd one.

He could not simply dismiss Christianity as outdated. He *did* think it was outdated, and sometimes said so with grotesque vividness:

– The days of creeds are as dead and done with as days of Pterodactyls:[6]
– On a gloomy gusty afternoon, going up the steep incline through the trees behind the town they came upon a Calvary tottering to its fall; and as it rocked in the wind like a ship's mast Hardy thought that the crudely painted figure of Christ upon it seemed to writhe and cry in the twilight: 'Yes, Yes!

I agree that this travesty of me and my doctrines should totter and overturn in this modern world !"[7]

But it is clear from this very passage – from the way the scene haunted Hardy – that he could not put Christianity out of his mind. Partly this was because, questions of belief apart, he found the church so fascinating as an institution. He even described himself as 'churchy':

> – not in an intellectual sense, but in so far as instincts and emotions ruled. As a child, to be a parson had been his dream; moreover, he had had several clerical relatives who held livings; while his grandfather, father, uncle, brother, wife, cousin, and two sisters had been musicians in various churches over a period covering altogether more than a hundred years. He himself had frequently read the church lessons, and had at one time as a young man begun reading for Cambridge with a view to taking Orders.[8]

Hardy also had strong theological interests: hence we find him constantly tampering with Christianity, even wondering if it can be restated in a way that will be compatible with modern agnosticism. He claimed that theist and atheist held almost identical ideas on the First Cause, only one called it God and the other no-God: Leslie Stephen (whose ideas influenced Hardy greatly) had made the same point in his *Agnostic's Apology*. Hence his hope in the 1920s that the Church of England would revise its Liturgy in a way that would 'include the majority of thinkers of the previous hundred years who had lost all belief in the supernatural'[9] – an odd hope then, and soon dashed, though it could be claimed that something like this has now begun to happen.

In formulating his views on man's place in the world, then, Hardy did not ignore Christianity: he attacked it, he mocked it, he worried at it, but could not leave it alone. The result is often very effective:

> We enter church, and we have to say, "We have erred and strayed from Thy ways like lost sheep", when what we want to say is, "Why are we made to err and stray like lost sheep?" Then we have to sing, "My soul doth magnify the Lord", when what we want to sing is, "O that my soul could find some Lord that it could magnify! Till it can, let us magnify

good works, and develop all means of easing mortals' progress through a world not worthy of them."[10]

This pessimistic philosophy is expressed in some of Hardy's most interesting poems. For a direct statement of it, we can turn to the opening chorus of his epic-drama *The Dynasts*. There we find that the force which moves history is like clockwork, controlling events heedlessly and without awareness. This force is known as the Immanent Will; and when the Spirit of the Pities protests at its rigid indifference to man's welfare, its unconsciousness of what it is doing, the Spirit of the Years, whose task is to behold what happens without feeling 'with or against', replies that there is no sign of the Immanent Will attaining an awareness of good and evil:

Rather they show that, like a knitter drowsed,
Whose fingers play in skilled unmindfulness,
The Will has woven with an absent heed
Since life first was; and ever will so weave.

Here clearly is the indifferent universe Hardy so often spoke of. Perhaps it is surprising that he calls the directing force 'the Immanent Will', and some critics have seen in this the influence of Schopenhauer.

Arthur Schopenhauer's great work, *Die Welt as Wille und Vorstellung*, which was first published in 1818, was perhaps the central text of nineteenth-century pessimism, and we know that Hardy had read at least some of Schopenhauer. Briefly, Schopenhauer offers two alternative modes of apprehending the world. The first – the world as representation, or idea, is the work of the intellect, and is subject to Kant's principle of sufficient reason, that space, time and causality, the categories by which we represent the world, do not belong to the thing in itself, but are the forms of our knowing, imposed by us on the world. But instead of coming to the sceptical conclusion that the world as it is in itself cannot be known, he postulates a different mode of apprehending it, the world as will, which is a blind, irresistible urge, the will-to-live, in which the individual is unimportant, and in which Nature lives in an eternal present (for past and future are temporal concepts dependent on the principle of sufficient reason). The most eloquent part of

Schopenhauer's philosophy is his demonstration that because the will is constantly striving all life is suffering; permanent gratification is impossible. Schopenhauer wrote before Darwin, and though his pessimism can obviously combine with some of the consequences of *The Origin of Species*, he rests his view that Nature is indifferent to the individual on a pre-Darwinian picture of the immutability of species, against which the helplessness of the individual life is vividly shown.

The most convenient statement of Hardy's pessimism is probably the opening chorus of *The Dynasts,* where he sets out to show the insignificance of the individual against the forces that control the Universe. Indeed, that is its trouble, poetically: it is so convenient a statement that we seem to be reading nothing more than a versification of the author's philosophy. Only one detail shows a verbal liveliness that takes us away from mere exposition. After the Chorus of the Pities has said they dare not hold the Immanent Will to be so utterly automatic, the Spirit of the Years replies:

Hold what ye list, fond unbelieving Sprites,
You cannot swerve the pulsion of the Byss,
Which thinking on, yet weighing not Its thought,
Unchecks Its clock-like laws.

The nicely ironic touch here is, of course, 'unbelieving'. Hardy has neatly reversed the traditional theology: now it is the wish to find moral purpose in Nature which is dismissed by the remorselessly authoritative spirit as 'unbelieving'. Here, surely, is the promise for a special kind of artistry: the artistry of agnosticism, we might say. The way to write an unChristian poem that is not mere assertion, we see, is to take some of the traditional commonplaces and visibly to upset them.

This is a promise which in a handful of poems Hardy magnificently fulfilled – poems of a twisted irony that exactly corresponds to the twist given to traditional theology.

Before Life and After
A time there was – as one may guess
And as, indeed, earth's testimonies tell –
Before the birth of consciousness,
When all went well.

None suffered sickness, love, or loss,
None knew regret, starved hope, or heart-burnings;
None cared whatever crash or cross
Brought wrack to things.

If something ceased, no tongue bewailed,
If something winced and waned, no heart was wrung;
If brightness dimmed, and dark prevailed,
No sense was stung.

But the disease of feeling germed,
And primal rightness took the tinct of wrong;
Ere nescience shall be reaffirmed
How long, how long?

The philosophy here is certainly that of Schopenhauer, where-ever Hardy got it from. The first edition of *The World as Will and Representation* ends with a celebration of Nirvana, of 'that peace which is higher than all reason, that ocean-like calmness of the spirit', that is so tempting to the man longing to escape from the restlessness of the constant activity of the will.

But poetry is not philosophy; and a true poet does not merely versify a philosophical position. Hardy's poem is controlled by one central invention, an imaginative act that translates the idea into poetic form. This is his use of the conventions of pastoral, presenting the original era of nothingness as a Golden Age. The line 'When all went well' introduces this, and the second stanza, taken on its own, could be from a description of Arcadia in a pastoral idyll, protected from the jealousies of court and the harshness of the world outside. The third stanza continues this tone, applying it more specifically to the time before the birth of consciousness. The final stanza is enlivened by some of Hardy's linguistic idiosyncrasy ('germed', or the unusual paradox of affirming nescience); and it presents the end of that primal calm as an act of destruction, analagous to the destruction of an Arcadian retreat. The result is a brilliant parody of the Creation, a literary device turned to the purpose of expounding a philosophical position.

So much for Hardy's pessimism, and its poetic expression. But pessimism is not the whole of his philosophy, for he also held a doctrine which he called meliorism – briefly, the doctrine that things will get better. We even find him referring in 1907 to 'the general growth of human altruism noticeable everywhere'. Some of his 'melioristic' statements however sound quite as gloomy as his pessimism:

> Altruism, or The Golden Rule, or whatever 'Love your Neighbour as Yourself' may be called, will ultimately be brought about I think by the pain we see in others reacting on ourselves, as if we and they were part of one body.[11]

It is hard not to suspect something dutiful about a meliorism which has to be squeezed out of such a Darwinian development.[12]

There are strong qualifications, too, to Hardy's meliorism. It was dented, perhaps destroyed, by the Great War, which, we are told, 'destroyed all his belief in the gradual ennoblement of man', and certainly there is a note of near-despair in his statements during and just after the War. This is not of course very relevant to his writing, since almost everything of importance had by then been written. But earlier remarks suggest that his hopefulness was of a very general, very long-term nature – indeed, to see what it was like we can turn to the final scene of *The Dynasts,* in which The Spirit of the Years once more debates with the Pities, but this time they persist in their hope that the Immanent Will may attain to a consciousness of purpose, that Its heart will awake 'In a genial germing purpose, and for loving-kindness' sake'; for if this should never happen humanity might as well 'darkle to extinction swift and sure.' Here is the final chorus:

> But – a stirring thrills the air
> Like to sounds of joyance there
> That the rages
> Of the ages
> Shall be cancelled, and deliverance offered from the darts that were,
> Consciousness the Will informing, till It fashion all things fair!

To read Hardy's poems in the light of his philosophy is natural and, at times, illuminating; but we can't run away from the fact that when this was done in his lifetime he protested strongly. One of the most interesting protests comes in a correspondence with Alfred Noyes,[13] who had said in a lecture that Hardy's philosophy saw the Power behind the Universe as an imbecile jester. Hardy's answer made two points. First, that there is a 'vast difference between the expression of fancy and the expression of belief'; and he then discusses the particular poems Noyes had cited in support of his view, maintaining that it would be wrong to deduce his actual beliefs from them. One poem is just 'an amusing instance of early cynicism'; another is spoken by a lover 'and lovers are chartered irresponsible'; another contains a Virgilian reminiscence; others contain 'legitimate imagery all of a piece with such expressions as "Life, Time's fool" . . . and I am amazed that you should see any *belief* in them'. And second, he states as his 'sober opinion' that the cause of Things 'is neither moral nor immoral, but unmoral: "loveless and hateless" I have called it, "which neither good nor evil knows" '. Both these points need discussing.

What is striking about the first is how literally Hardy seems to treat the charge ('people will go on thinking that I really believe the Prime Mover to be a malignant old gentleman, a sort of King of Dahomey'). He is so anxious to deny that sort of belief, that he seems to consider his 'sober beliefs' more important than his 'fancies'.

It is only a short step from this to regarding poetry as a trivial amusement, and Hardy almost seems to take it. But of course the world would have little interest in Hardy's sober beliefs if he had written no poems (we shall come to the novels later) – he would be at most a minor example in the history of Victorian agnosticism. In fact we know that Hardy took poetry very seriously; but he does not seem to allow that the writing of a poem may explore more deeply into a man's beliefs than a direct statement of them, and that the philosophy implicit in his poetry may be more truly his than what he states in sober prose. Of course it will be an 'as if' philosophy: it is easy to reassure him that we know there is no King of Dahomey in the sky. But if it shapes the poems it may correspond to the profoundest level of his being.

What then *is* the operative philosophy of Hardy's writing; is it that the Cause of Things is neither moral nor immoral but unmoral? If it derives fom Darwin, this is what we would expect: a Cause that takes the form of objective natural laws,

47

perceived by the scientist. If it derives from the rich despair of Schopenhauer, the keen sense of human suffering, we may be less sure. And here it is time to mention that the dialogues in the Overworld that begin and end *The Dynasts* do not take place only between Pity and the Spirit of the Years; there is also a Spirit Ironic and a Spirit Sinister. After the Spirit of the Years has spoken of the clock-like laws of the Immanent Will, the Spirit Sinister remarks (aside):

Good, as before.
My little engines, then, will still have play.

Now if the clock-like proceedings of the Immanent Will leave no scope for Pity to interfere, why should they leave any scope for these 'Little engines' of malice? Hardy has already told us in the Preface that only the Spirit of the Pities corresponds to 'the Universal Sympathy of human nature – the spectator idealised'. The Spirits Ironic and Sinister, then, have some more objective status than Pity has, and those engines are in some way operating. The Cause of Things, it seems, is not altogether unmoral.

I shall not follow this discussion any further into the poetry: my purpose was simply to show that in moving from the philosophy to its literary expression we must not allow ourselves to be bullied by the author. The philosophy he claims to hold as sober belief will no doubt resemble, but it may not be identical with, the philosophy that is actually embedded in his work. If this is a complex issue in the poems, it is even more complex in the novels, to which it is now high time we turned.

* * *

We have seen that three readings of Hardy's philosophy are possible. There is meliorism; there is the indifference of a universe that knows nothing of morality; and there is (the phrase is too good to drop) the King-of-Dahomey view, that postulates a positive vindictiveness in things, a Spirit Sinister actively at work.

Now first of all we must say that there is little or no meliorism in the novels. It would be a highly eccentric reading of them which saw them as statements on how the human lot is improving, how there is 'a growth of human altruism noticeable everywhere.' It is not only the deeply tragic endings of the greatest novels; even in those which end more or less happily there are qualifications – the chastened happiness of Gabriel Oak finally marrying Bathsheba will not, we feel, ever efface the profounder sorrow she has been through; Grace's final reunion with Fitz-piers will soon be shadowed by his continuing infidelities. In-deed, we may ask how the novels *could* express meliorism, since that doctrine is so long-term in its operation. A gradual move for the better in the sorrowful lot of man is unlikely to manifest itself in the particular story of misunderstanding and disappoint-ment acted out in front of us.

What contemporary readers did find in them was often, in fact, the King-of-Dahomey view. Complaints of Hardy's pessi-mism began to be made with the publication of *The Return of the Native* (1878) and *The Mayor* (1886), and reached their climax with *Tess* and *Jude*. Reviewers of *Tess*, even those who admired it, spoke of it as gloomy, as painful, as sounding a depth of unrelieved, relentless darkness, as pagan and even blasphe-mous. R. H. Hutton complained in *The Spectator* that it illustrated the conviction:

that not only is there no Providence guiding individual men and women in the right way, but that, in many cases at least, there is something like a malign fate which draws them out of the right way into the wrong way.[14]

There were even stronger complaints, which roused Hardy's objections, such as that he

postulates an all-powerful being endowed with the baser human passions, who turns everything to evil and rejoices in the mischief he has wrought.[15]

What is there in the novel to give a sense of such intense, even perverse gloom? We can begin from two of its most famous remarks, one near the beginning, one right at the end. When Tess is driving the wagon with her young brother Abraham in Chapter V, he asks her about the stars, and whether it is true that they are worlds:

'Yes.'
'All like ours?'
'I don't know; but I think so. They sometimes seem to be

like the apples on our stubbard-tree. Most of them splendid and sound – a few blighted.'

'Which do we live on – a splendid one or a blighted one?'

'A blighted one.'

Even more famous is the remark that ends the book. After Tess has been executed, and the black flag is raised on the tower of the jail, Hardy writes:

'Justice' was done, and the President of the Immortals, in Aeschylean phrase, had ended his sport with Tess.

It seems perfectly understandable that the critics should have commented on Hardy's evident belief in an all-powerful and malicious being, who rejoices in the mischief he has wrought; and the opinion has persisted to our own time. There is not really much difference between the indignation of contemporary readers and the more jaunty complaint made in more modern terminology by William Empson:

To believe in a spirit who only jeers at you is superstitious without having any of the advantages of superstition; besides, it has a sort of petty wilfulness, it comes of trying to think of something nasty to say.[16]

We can guess by now the nature of Hardy's reply. He gives the highly literal interpretation to 'believe' we have already seen, and complains that the use of the well-known trope of personification is not to be taken as revealing a sober belief in a man-shaped tribal god, or celestial King of Dahomey. And we can of course accept this, while at the same time feeling that the trope may tell us more than sober prose. And we have incidentally found a name for the King of Dahomey: he is, we noticed, the President of the Immortals, and he comes from Greek Tragedy. Of this, more shortly.

Let us agree then to leave sober belief out of it, now that we have got to the novels. It is in any case a tricky matter with Hardy, who alternated between tendentious statements of belief and excessive shyness about having his own opinions discussed. Let us speak instead of the beliefs implicit in the novels. We cannot of course interpret a novel wholly by means of a couple of philosophical remarks however vivid, however subsequently famous; we need to ask whether they do in fact represent the spirit of the book.

Tess's remark is after all dramatic – made not by the author but by a character, who has some reason to feel discouraged, as she reflects on her father's fecklessness and her brother's embarrassing suggestions that their rich relation is going to help her to marry a gentleman. True, we know that the author had himself made similar remarks – one very similar indeed, when he wrote in his journal (7 April 1889) 'This planet does not supply the materials for happiness to higher existence. Other planets may, though one can hardly see how'.[17] But what is much more important is that Tess's remark is almostly immediately confirmed by what happens. Her brother goes to sleep and she falls into a reverie in which she sees the landscape round her as if in a Hardy poem: 'the occasional heave of the wind became the sigh of some immense sad soul, conterminous with the universe in space, and with history in time'. She is startled out of this by a sudden jerk, and finds that she has dropped asleep and allowed the wagon to move to the wrong side of the road, and that the mail cart has collided with her, and driven its pointed shaft into the breast of her father's poor old horse Prince, who is dying. This means ruin for the Durbeyfield family, whose world is certainly blighted now.

The remark about the President of the Immortals is more prominently placed than Tess's reflection, and is given in the author's own person. To confirm it we look, not forward to one particular event, but backward to the whole book, and ask whether what we have been shown is indeed Tess being made sport of by forces too great for her to control. So vivid a concluding paragraph ought, certainly, to sum up the book: if it doesn't we are being misled, and for the sake of a startling phrase the ending has been unbalanced. For this is of course the way to treat authorial comment and conclusion: not to assume that it correctly describes the book as a whole, but to ask whether it does – and to feel rather cheated if it doesn't.

Now there is certainly a great deal in *Tess* that does suggest she is a victim of cruelly conspiring circumstances. The greatest disaster in her life is the fact that when she makes her confession to Angel on their wedding day, he reacts with such priggish shock, such virtuous horror, that he is unable to accept her as his wife. The reasons for this are complex. Partly, they are to be found in Angel's character – a man of advanced intellectual and religious views, who is more in the grip of convention on sexual matters than we (or perhaps he) had realised. Angel's virtuous harshness is accentuated by the fact that he has committed the same offence, and in fact it is his confession to her that at last unleashes the confession she has been longing and dreading to make to him. Now on one level Hardy is here making a straightforward social point, a criticism of the double standard, that regards sexual offences as venial in a man, but grave in a woman; and in so far as the cause is social it is not the work of the President of the Immortals but of man, and can be remedied. Yet even this point, if seen as part of the developing action, fits into the series of details that make sport of Tess. For a long time she refuses to marry Clare, believing that she is too sullied by her previous seduction ever to be his wife; and even after she has agreed she makes constant but unsuccessful attempts to confess to him. The overwhelming impression which this part of the book leaves is that everything conspired to prevent her telling. Before she has accepted him she manages to say, on one occasion, 'I will tell you my experiences – all about myself – all!' and in reply he drops the note of passionate pleading he has been using, and turns to banter – 'My Tess has, no doubt, almost as many experiences as that wild convolvulus out there', thus making it all the harder for her to go on. When they are driving together after delivering the milk, and she is pressed into explaining why she keeps refusing him, they pass the ruins of an old manor house that had once belonged to the d'Urbervilles, and he talks to her about the decline of the family, thus enabling her, when it comes to confessing her secret, to say that she is a d'Urberville not a Durbeyfield – unwittingly, he has himself offered her the way of escape from truth. Angel Clare decides they had better be married by licence, not by the calling of banns, thus removing another possibility of the truth being revealed. At breakfast one morning the dairyman tells the story of Jack Dollop who married a widow for her money, not knowing that she lost it on remarrying, and this sparks off a discussion on what a wife should tell her husband before marriage – from which Tess escapes in embarrassment and distress. Shopping in the near-by town she is recognised by a man from Trantridge, whose reaction might have given the secret away to Angel Clare, if Angel had not been quick-tempered and the man cautious. And then finally, after all these narrow escapes, Tess sits down and writes a confession which she slips under the door of Angel's room – but it goes under the carpet, and he does not see it.

What does all this add up to? Over and over, the secret is on the verge of coming out, and then something intervenes. Tess herself is to blame, of course: she loves Angel passionately, and is terrified of losing him. But how elaborately she is helped by circumstances – or rather, not helped but hindered, since in the event her trouble comes from her not having told Angel. The letter under the carpet is the last straw: after that we cannot (surely) question that the President of the Immortals is sporting with Tess.

It is not only in terms of plot that we can test the validity of the final paragraph as a summary of what the book is saying. Sometimes there is in the language itself a sense of not being altogether at ease in the world, an awareness of the richness and fertility of nature that is at the same time aware that the universe was not designed for man to be comfortable in. For instance:

> The outskirt of the garden in which Tess found herself had been left uncultivated for some years, and was now damp and rank with juicy grass which sent up mists of pollen at a touch; and with tall blooming weeds emitting offensive smells – weeds whose red and yellow and purple hues formed a polychrome as dazzling as that of cultivated flowers. She went stealthily as a cat through this profusion of growth, gathering cuckoo-spittle on her skirts, cracking snails that were underfoot, staining her hands with thistle-milk and slug-slime, and rubbing off upon her naked arms sticky blights which, though snow-white on the apple-tree trunks, made madder stains on her skin; thus she drew quite near to Clare, still unobserved of him.

Richness, fertility – but also corruption. Nature does not altogether welcome Tess in this neglected garden, will not quite leave her clean. Some of the details are put in a way that almost startles:

The light which still shone was derived mainly from a large hole in the western bank of cloud; it was like a piece of day left behind by accident, dusk having closed in elsewhere.

It is as if Hardy had deliberately set out to denude evening of its associations, reducing it to a monotonous and utterly mechanical occurrence. The rift in the cloud is merely a hole, the very presence of light is merely an accident. This impression is conveyed directly by the description, but some of it is present in Tess's consciousness; and when she falls into conversation with Clare she blends what may be a reminiscence of Macbeth with a curiously matter-of-fact, even eerie effect:

And you seem to see numbers of to-morrows just all in a line, the first of them the biggest and clearest, the others getting smaller and smaller as they stand farther away; but they all seem very fierce and cruel and as if they said, 'I'm coming! Beware of me! Beware of me!'

The mixture of abstract and concrete is very startling here. Tess speaks of the tomorrows with great familiarity, as of well-known objects (or even people), yet she does nothing to describe them or in any way suggest what they look like. The effect, it seems to me, is of someone astonishingly aware of her own experience – experience we can't share with her and that she is uneasy about. When she reports her feeling of alienation she seems to know what she is talking about.

'A writer's work should be judged as a whole', wrote Hardy to Alfred Noyes, 'and not picked passages that contradict them as a whole.' If we are to judge *Tess of the d'Urbervilles* as a whole, it will surely not be misleading to say that the heroine inhabits a hostile world and is the sport of malignant powers.

*　　*　　*

I now turn back to *The Mayor*; and here too we can begin with an explicit statement about the ingenious machinery contrived by the gods for our harm. It comes in Chapter XLIV, when Henchard has left Casterbridge to avoid the returning Newson, leaving Elizabeth-Jane with whom he is now reconciled, and returns to his original trade of hay-trussing:

And thus Henchard found himself again on the precise standing which he had occupied a quarter of a century before. Externally there was nothing to hinder his making another start on the upward slope, and by his new lights achieving higher things than his soul in its half-formed state had been able to accomplish. But the ingenious machinery contrived by the Gods for reducing human possibilities of amelioration to a minimum – which arranges that wisdom to do shall come *pari passu* with the departure of zest for doing – stood in the way of all that. He had no wish to make an arena a second time of a world that had become a mere painted scene to him.

We seem to be back again with the President of the Immortals; and in his review of *The Mayor* R. H. Hutton complained that it contained too much 'fashionable pessimism'. Quoting this passage, he gave an objection that is both orthodox and intelligent. The true purpose of 'human possibilities of amelioration' he maintained, is an inner-amelioration, an improvement of character, that does not need the further confirmation of earthly success. 'What Mr Hardy calls "the ingenious machinery contrived by the gods for reducing human possibilities of amelioration to a minimum," appears to us to be the means taken by the moral wisdom which overrules our fate for showing us that the use of characters is not to mould circumstances, but rather that it is the use of circumstance to chasten and purify character'.[18] This could not be said of *Tess*: for there is no more suggestion there that Tess is the better for her ordeals than that the hare is better for being hunted. Henchard, in contrast, does grow morally, and is in some way a wiser man (though also a broken man) for what he has been through. The ingenious machinery has not been as cruel to him as the President was to Tess; and even what it has done – take away his zest for doing, so that he cannot climb back to what he was – is done through him. By operating upon his character, rather than upon him through circumstances, this machinery seems to have less of an independant existence than Fate or the King of Dahomey, it seems to be more like an account of what men are like than a constraint imposed upon them.

But once again we must move from particular passages like

this to the total impact of the novel, and ask whether the plot confirms such remarks. And on the plot of *The Mayor* there is a good deal to say. Fate, as we have seen, operates through plot in a novel, and takes the form of chance – i.e. of those events which we could not have foreseen by observing what went before, for they seem caused neither by the intention of the main character, nor by the probable outcome of earlier actions. We refer something to chance when we did not expect it and cannot explain it. Now ill chance can operate in different ways in a plot. It can fall on all alike, innocent or guilty: that is the pattern that would correspond to Hardy's indifferent universe, his Cause that is neither moral nor immoral, but unmoral. Or it can perform a kind of moral function, either by punishing the guilty when they least expect it, or at least by showing that we are somehow responsible for our own destiny: this is the pattern traditionally known as poetic justice, and of course it implies a just or at least a rational power controlling the world. Or it can behave like the Spirits Ironic and Sinister, and single out the innocent, as it partly seems to do in *Tess*.

There are glimpses of the Spirit Ironic in *The Mayor*, as we have seen, but they are rare. Indeed, we happen to know that Hardy removed some. This is the one novel which he revised after serial publication – not just to the extent of restoring passages which the primness of magazine readers had required him to omit, as happened with several of his other novels, but a real revision that added and removed episodes for the sake of artistic effect. And in the serial version, Henchard marries Lucetta just before the return of Susan into his life. When telling Farfrae his story, in Chapter XII, he describes how Lucetta saved his life when he fell out of a boat in the harbour, and how he married her in gratitude; and Farfrae is involved in a more active capacity than that of simply giving advice, since he rides to Budmouth to deliver a letter – which he has himself written for Henchard – to Lucetta as she arrives on the packet from Jersey. There were greater complications too over the failure to return Lucetta's letters when she passed through Casterbridge – the packet passes through almost everyone's hands and there is even a meeting between Lucetta and Susan. Much of this is so elaborate as to be clumsy, and in simplifying the episodes and removing much of the melodrama, Hardy certainly improved his novel; and at the same time he diminished the impression of a series of unlucky chances conspiring against Henchard, or amusing itself by narrowly avoiding trouble. He did not however completely remove this, and in the final version the letters become public because Henchard, with surprising casualness, entrusts them to Jopp.[19]

The opposite view – chance as operating with a kind of poetic justice – is by no means absent from *The Mayor*. The powerful figure of Henchard stays in our minds as one who acts quite as much as he is acted upon, and results which we are at first inclined to attribute to chance turn out, on reflection, to be indirectly due to him. We have already seen one example of this in the weather, where I suggested that what ruined Henchard was not so much the sudden bad harvests as the nature of his own decisions; and the story is full of similar examples. Over and over, circumstances conspire against Henchard in a way that seems sheer bad luck; but what they do is permit the consequences of his own rashness to take place when with common good luck they might have been avoided. Henchard's attempt to fetch Farfrae back to look after the dying Lucetta fails because Farfrae will not believe him – not surprising, since Henchard has just come close to murdering him. Unlucky, surely, that these two events came one after the other: but how can you expect the Spirit Ironic to forego such juxtapositions, if you are the kind of man who behaves as Henchard does? Henchard's deception of Newson, sending him away by saying Elizabeth-Jane is dead, was not as premeditated, not as callous, as Elizabeth-Jane believes – it is his bad luck that the version she comes to believe omits all the extenuations: but the man who is such a mixture of pride and impulse is not likely to defend himself, and Henchard's silence allows the Spirit Sinister to get away with Its contrivances. What we are seeing here is an old and celebrated literary device: the unlikely outcome that brings about what we somehow feel to be the logical, the appropriate (even if the cruelly unjust) consequence of a character's deeds. Perhaps the most famous example of it is in *King Lear*. What is striking in this play is the enormity of the suffering of Lear and Gloucester. Why are Gloucester's eyes put out? Is it just the savagery of Cornwall and Regan, combined with Gloucester's bad luck, or is he himself somehow responsible? Both views are canvassed in the play. The view that the innocent suffer through a malignant cruelty in the nature of things – the King-of-Dahomey view – has never been so memorably stated as in Gloucester's lines:

As flies to wanton boys are we to the gods.
They kill us for their sport.

On the other hand, there is a case that Gloucester brought it on himself. It is stated with shocking crudity by Edgar:

The Gods are just, and of our pleasant vices
Make instruments to plague us.
The dark and vicious place where thee he got
Cost him his eyes.

If Gloucester had not committed adultery there would have been no Edmund, in which case – well, in which case he might still have lost his eyes, since it was not Edmund who blinded him. It would be so painful to accept these lines as true (is there *no* proportion between crime and punishment?) that it is a relief to have good reason for rejecting them, and for taking 'just' ironically (Edgar's irony, or Shakespeare's?). But there is a more defensible sense in which Gloucester was responsible for what happened. He could not judge which of his sons was the honest man; a prey to superstition, he let Edmund make a fool of him; he did not have the courage to resist Cornwall and the sisters until it was too late – over and over, Gloucester emerges as a weak character, and we live in a cruel world that punishes the weak. It is not justice, but it is a kind of logic.

A parallel example of a man's deeds coming home to roost is that of Henchard and the furmity woman. Here again, he had bad luck: she turned up in Casterbridge on the one day when he happened to be presiding as magistrate, and so was able to disgrace him publicly. But all that this bad luck did was enable Henchard to be confronted with the truth of his own action in a way that does not often happen in the untidiness of life. Chance – or the Spirit Ironic – contrived the exposure, but the subject matter itself came from Henchard.

Here Henchard looks more like Lear than Gloucester; the parallel with Lear has struck many critics. The opening scenes are strikingly similar: a rash, headstrong man commits an act of folly, involving the repudiation of a woman. He brushes aside all warnings, and imposes his will; we know he will regret it, and though we cannot help partly identifying with his enormous energy, we suspect that he is setting something in motion that will destroy him. Lear clearly does this. If the opening scene of *The Mayor* is not so crucial, it is because of the episodic nature of the plot that I have already discussed: the return of the furmity woman is only one of a whole series of downward steps in Henchard's career, and Hardy's remark that that day constituted the turning point in his fortunes, after which everything declined steadily, sounds like an attempt to attribute to his novel more of the structure of retribution than it has.

There are other resemblances, and Abel Whittle plays a role that has much of the Fool in it. But my purpose in drawing the parallel is not so much to point to similarities between the two men, as to those between the two works. For one way in which we have not yet considered *The Mayor* is as a tragedy, yet this may be the aspect that most profoundly expresses Hardy's philosophy.

* * *

Modern theories of tragedy have usually stressed above all the fact that the tragic hero is responsible for what happens to him. We owe to Aristotle the term 'recognition' (anagnorisis) for the climax of a tragedy, though the meaning has changed in modern criticism. In Aristotle it refers to the recognition of an intellectual mistake; in the theory of Bradley (and in the practice of Shakespeare) it refers to the discovery of a moral flaw, the realisation 'Look what I've done' or 'Am I like that?' If the pattern of tragedy is the noble but flawed hero unleashing a terrible action that in some way destroys him, but not before he has attained recognition, then the opposite of tragedy will be an action in which the hero is not responsible, in which there is nothing he need understand, for understanding could not alter what happened, and in which the suffering reveals neither justice nor even necessarily logic. Robert Heilman calls this the literature of disaster:

> In disaster, what happens comes from without; in tragedy, from within. In disaster, we are victims; in tragedy, we make

59

victims, of others or of ourselves. In disaster, our moral quality, though it may be revealed, is secondary; in tragedy, it is primary, the very source of all that happens.[20]

Heilman points out that in popular usage, disaster is often called tragedy: a young man hits a lorry parked on a highway, he and his fiancée are killed, and the newspapers report it as 'Tragedy on Highway 40':

> 'Tragedy on Highway 40' lacks the active participation by the characters, the exercise of choice, the awareness of options as equal or better or worse, the knowledge of self.[21]

The view that Heilman rejects is very close to that which Jean Anouilh accepts in his version of *Antigone*. The Chorus of Anouilh's play is a thoughtful critic who points out that both Antigone and Creon are victims of their temperament and their situation, so that there is never any doubt about how they are going to act; and who claims that what makes such a play tragic is the quality of the characters' response to a situation that is imposed on them:

> Tragedy is clean, it is restful, it is flawless. It has nothing to do with melodrama – with wicked villains, persecuted maidens, avengers, sudden revelations and eleventh-hour repentances. Death, in a melodrama, is really horrible because it is never inevitable. The dear old father might so easily have been saved; the honest young man might so easily have brought in the police five minutes earlier.
>
> In a tragedy, nothing is in doubt and everyone's destiny is known. That makes for tranquillity. There is a sort of fellow-feeling among characters in a tragedy: he who kills is as innocent as he who gets killed: it's all a matter of what part you are playing. Tragedy is restful; and the reason is that hope, that foul, deceitful thing, has no part in it. There isn't any hope. You're trapped. The whole sky has fallen on you, and all you can do about it is to shout.
>
> Don't mistake me: I said 'shout'. I did not say groan, whimper, complain. That, you cannot do. But you can shout aloud: you can get all those things said that you never thought you'd be able to say – or never even knew you had it in you to say.

By Heilman's view this is melodrama (the term he uses to describe the drama of disaster), for Antigone is not in conflict with herself, but with other men or the world. The essential element of tragedy for Heilman, that the hero should be divided, so that he will be able to recognise in himself an element of responsibility for the action, is not even considered by Anouilh; for him, the contrast is between defying and accepting (meekly or cringingly) a destiny over which one has no control.

The choice between these two conceptions of tragedy is a choice of philosophies. Heilman's conception is often defended as showing the clear-sightedness of tragedy, the fact that it evades nothing, but forces the tragic hero to see what his actions led to, and us to see what, in the clear glass of tragic contrivance, our actions might lead to. But it is also possible to argue that this sort of tragedy is the supreme kind of self-deception: in a world in which no individual can control the forces that operate on him, what a comfort it is to be told that even the most terrible catastrophes are somehow brought about by ourselves.

Holders of each of these theories of tragedy will naturally tend to choose different plays to support their thesis; but the one play either party might choose is *King Lear*. It is so profoundly and puzzlingly concerned with divine justice, with whether the gods do persecute us malignantly, that it is very possible to see its gods as (in Hardyesque phrase) the President of the Immortals. But on the other hand the tremendous impact made by Lear in the opening scene seems to place him before us as a man determined to control his own destiny, to the point of self-destruction.

And now the parallel with Hardy can be stated very simply. If *King Lear* is seen as an Anouilh-type tragedy, it is like *Tess*, who was like a fly to that wanton President; but if it is seen as a Heilman-type tragedy it is like *The Mayor*, who acted more than he was acted on, and for whom the role of those contriving gods was to spell out the full consequences.

* * *

In a world indifferent to man, expectations must be pitched low and suffering endured without complaint. This ethical attitude is sometimes called Stoic and some readers have felt they perceived it in Hardy's novels; though it can never really be correct to describe any of Hardy's characters as a Stoic, since the metaphysical basis of Stoicism is so utterly different from his. The ancient Stoics saw the universe as rationally ordered; although cruel fortune might befall us in everyday life, the ultimate principles governing the world were rational, and virtue therefore was the exercise of Right Reason; whereas reason in Hardy's world is more likely to lead you to defy the indifferent or even hostile powers that govern it.

In a loose popular sense, the old shepherd waiting to be hired at the Casterbridge fair might be called Stoical:

> He was evidently a chastened man. The battle of life had been a sharp one with him, for, to begin with, he was a man of small frame. He was now so bowed by hard work and years that, approaching from behind, a person could hardly see his head. He had planted the stem of his crook in the gutter, and was resting upon the bow, which was polished to silver brightness by the long friction of his hands. He had quite forgotten where he was, and what he had come for, his eyes being bent on the ground. (Chapter XXIII.)

In the event, the battle of life is kind to the old man in this chapter, for Farfrae (partly to please Lucetta) hires him along with his son, thus avoiding a separation of the sweethearts. As far as plot is concerned, shepherd and son only appear in the book so that Farfrae can resolve their problem; but they have already made their own impression before he sees them, and it is one of the dogged acceptance of suffering – so that it is not surprising to learn that the sketch was originally written for his essay *The Dorsetshire Labourer*, and subsequently inserted into the novel.

Avoiding the term Stoic, let us speak of a philosophy of quiet acceptance of one's lot, an awareness of suffering which teaches one to avoid the excessive emotions of joy and fear, pity and sorrow. The representative of such an attitude in *The Mayor* is clearly Elizabeth-Jane. It is she who 'had learnt the lesson of renunciation, and was as familiar with the wreck of each day's wishes as with the diurnal setting of the sun'; it is she who articulates most clearly the philosophy that Henchard's sufferings might lead to. Elizabeth-Jane suffers, but for her things end well; and in directing attention to her story and her feelings at the end, Hardy sets out to reconcile the fact of happiness and the philosophy of suffering. The result is a very puzzling conclusion.

After Elizabeth-Jane's life settles into equable serenity, she is able to teach others 'the secret (as she had once learned it) of making limited opportunities endurable.' Even if that secret is no longer so necessary to her, she can still serve the function of helping others in greater distress than herself to practise it. Hardy does not explore the implications of this, which sounds distressingly like a habit by someone in prosperity of telling the poor and the miserable that they must put up with their lot. What he does explore, however, in the very last paragraph, is the effect of the teaching on herself; and it is here that the real puzzlement comes:

> Her teaching had a reflex action upon herself, insomuch that she thought she could perceive no great personal difference between being respected in the nether parts of Casterbridge, and glorified at the uppermost end of the social world. Her position was, indeed, to a marked degree one that, in the common phrase, afforded much to be thankful for. That she was not demonstrably thankful was no fault of hers. Her experience had been of a kind to teach her, rightly or wrongly, that the doubtful honour of a brief transit through a sorry world hardly called for effusiveness, even when the path was suddenly irradiated at some half-way point by daybeams rich as hers. But her strong sense that neither she nor any human being deserved less than was given, did not blind her to the fact that there were others receiving less who had deserved much more. And in being forced to class herself among the fortunate she did not cease to wonder at the persistence of the unforeseen, when the one to whom such unbroken tranquillity had been accorded in the adult stage was she whose youth had seemed to teach that happiness was but the occasional episode in a general drama of pain. (Chapter XLV.)

Why is she not effusive at her good fortune? Because she fears it will not last, or because the taste of happiness has grown insipid to her? Her temperament may well incline her to the latter, but Hardy explicitly tells us that it is not her temperament but her experience that has taught her this lesson. The experience of seeing Henchard's ups and downs at such close quarters is more likely to have taught her the uncertainty of happiness than its tameness, but there is no hint that the tranquillity of her married life is anything but permanent. Hardy may have slipped into Elizabeth-Jane's consciousness here an awareness that would more properly belong to Henchard.

But the real puzzle comes in the last two sentences. The first is deeply pessimistic: if no human being deserves less than is given, the world must surely be governed by a cruel arrangement to make us unhappy. The second, however, turns to something like optimism: she had been wrong, then, in seeing happiness as 'but the occasional episode in a general drama of pain' – or had she? If Hardy wants us to reject this view, it is clumsy in the extreme to end the book with so memorable a statement of it. And the unexpected happiness has not led her to reflect on the presence of a benevolent design in things after all, merely 'to wonder at the persistence of the unforeseen.' If that is all it has done, we can see some significance in the startling expression 'being forced to class herself among the fortunate.' Hardy seems to be writing against the grain here: something in him – and he attributes it to Elizabeth-Jane too – does not want to renounce or even greatly modify his pessimism, so that the adjustments made to it under the pressure of the happy ending are limited and even grudging.

It is the most unsatisfactory ending of all Hardy's novels, and few readers remember it.[22] The ending that stays in the mind is Henchard's death only a page earlier to which this makes so inconclusive a postscript. Henchard, although he leaves Casterbridge with the rhetoric of Stoicism on his lips ('my punishment is *not* greater than I can bear') is even less of a Stoic, in the strict sense, than Elizabeth Jane. If his philosophy is one of acceptance, it is not quiet acceptance but something much more theatrical. It is a philosophy more appropriate to a tragic hero: and we ought now to look at Henchard in the light of his role as hero. In the first chapter, I discussed Henchard's character almost as if he had an independent existence as a human being. Suppose we shift the emphasis from the character to the book, as a total experience for the reader. We may then make the same points about Henchard, but they will be made differently, for we shall be looking at him as part of a design, asking what impact a certain kind of man will make on us, and how appropriate that impact is to the tragic experience.

What terminology best describes the tragic hero? It is common to speak of his pride, and it is obviously true that heroes as varied as Oedipus, Faustus, Othello and Lear all suffer from pride. This is true, and at the same time of limited value: any term that describes such varied persons must have a vast vague meaning. Yes, Henchard is proud, but not in the same way as Oedipus, who wants to drag all into the light and is ignorant, whereas Henchard conceals even what might help him, but speaks out, in his moment of truth, when publicly shamed; nor in the same way as Faustus, whose immoderate ambition was intellectual and remorseless, not personal and fitful; nor even, quite, in the same way as Lear (who loses his pride in the end). Another useful but very general term is 'uncompromising': the tragic hero is he who won't settle for half, won't admit he was wrong – or not until it is too late. As we reflect on the kind of man Henchard was, we see how well suited he is to the role of tragic hero – he is superstitious, for a sense of mysterious and not altogether understandable cosmic forces hovers round tragedy, and the hero is somehow in touch with them; and passionate, for reasonableness implies the ability to control and modify one's fate, and so to avoid the uncompromising end that the tragic hero faces directly.

One other characteristic of tragic form must be mentioned. The shape of the action is very important in tragedy. The series of disasters and suffering that the hero passes through will lead to a climax that must in some way seem a change, or at least a culmination for him. Once it has happened, there is no going back; and so it will usually come just before his death. This means that the ending of a tragedy is of special importance: there can be no feeling that things could continue, that the author has merely offered us a selection from an ongoing process. Tragedy is very different in structure from the slice of life of the chronicler.

The ending of *The Mayor* is without doubt crucial. It is not simply that Henchard dies (irreversible though that is), it is that our last glimpse of him sums up so much of what he stood for, with such concentrated power, that to watch him going on would be an anticlimax. Like so many tragic heroes, he dies for aesthetic reasons, after his final tremendous gesture. We may think the gesture was made possible by the impending death, but perhaps it is more faithful to the impact of the work to say that after such a gesture it would be anti-climax to go on living.

The death of Henchard is not, however, shown directly: he is given no curtain speech. It is described by Abel Whittle, in one of the most Shakespearean passages in Hardy, indeed in English fiction:

'Yes, ma'am he's gone! He was kind-like to mother when she wer here below, sending her the best ship-coal, and hardly any ashes from it at all; and taties, and suchlike that were very needful to her. I seed en go down street on the night of your worshipful's wedding to the lady at yer side, and I thought he looked low and faltering. And I followed en over Grey's Bridge, and he turned and zeed me, and said, "You go back!" But I followed, and he turned again, and said, "Do you hear, sir? Go back!" But I zeed that he was low, and I followed on still. Then 'a said, "Whittle, what do ye follow me for when I've told ye to go back all these times?" And I said, "Because, sir, I see things be bad with 'ee, and ye wer kind-like to mother if ye were rough to me, and would fain be kind-like to you." Then he walked on, and I followed; and he never complained at me no more. We walked on like that all night; and in the blue o' the morning, when 'twas hardly day, I looked ahead o' me, and I zeed that he wambled, and could hardly drag along. By that time we had got past here, but I had seen that this house was empty as I went by, and I got him to come back; and I took down the boards, from the windows, and helped him inside. "What, Whittle," he said, "and can ye really be such a poor fond fool as to care for such a wretch as I!" Then I went on further, and some neighbourly woodmen lent me a bed, and a chair, and a few other traps, and we brought 'em here, and made him as comfortable as we could. But he didn't gain strength, for you see, ma'am, he couldn't eat – no, no appetite at all – and he got weaker; and to-day he died. One of the neighbours have gone to get a man to measure him.' (Chapter XLV.)

I have already pointed out Whittle's resemblance to Lear's Fool, and some awareness of this must be present in the very moving line when Henchard refers to himself as a 'poor fond fool' – a reversal very similar to Lear's own when he wakes after his great rage and says:

> I am a very foolish fond old man
> Fourscore and upward, not an hour more or less,
> And to speak plainly
> I fear I am not in my perfect mind.

The striking difference between the two passages is of course that Lear says this after the Fool has gone out of his life, and Henchard says it *to* the Fool. Neither is better, and the contrast is significant: in both cases what we are seeing is a change of role, in Lear's it is internal, in Henchard's social

But *Lear* is not the only Shakespearean echo of this passage; it beautifully recalls the death of Falstaff, as described by the Hostess in *Henry V*:

> A' parted even just between twelve and one, even at the turning o' the tide. For after I saw him fumble with the sheets, and play with flowers, and smile upon his fingers' ends, I know there was but one way. For his nose was as sharp as a pen, and a' babbled of green fields. 'How now, Sir John!' quoth I. 'What, man! Be o' good cheer.' So a' cried 'God, God, God!' three or four times. Now I, to comfort him, bid him a' should not think of God, I hoped there was no need to trouble himself with any such thoughts yet. So a' bade me lay more clothes on his feet. I put my hand into the bed and felt them, and they were as cold as any stone. Then I felt to his knees, and they were as cold as any stone, and so upward and upward, and all was as cold as any stone. (Act II, Scene 3.)

In both passages, the death is measured against a time-keeping that is older than clocks: the turning of the tide in Shakespeare, the blue o' the morning in Hardy. In both we are being told of the break-up of a body – the mounting cold in Falstaff, the growing weakness in Henchard – by someone who feels inarticulately that the death is a spiritual loss too. In both the speaker is vividly characterised by the earthiness of the language – Whittle like a simple countryman conveys the kindness of Henchard to his mother by listing the things he gave her, very particularly ('the best ship-coal, and hardly any ashes from it at all') and he speaks in a dialect that sounds both authentic and poetic. For this is no mere literary imitation: it is a marvellous capturing of two contrasting voices, the rambling narrative of Whittle and out of it rising, loud and firm, the last shout of Henchard's pride: 'Do you hear, sir? Go back.' The pride is so intense that Henchard could never admit that it was broken; but the silent concession of Henchard walking on and never complaining no more is his true tragic defeat.

Henchard dies offstage; but it is not quite true that he has no curtain speech. His final soliloquy is his Will, and it is the most powerful ending of any Hardy character.

'MICHAEL HENCHARD'S WILL.

'That Elizabeth-Jane Farfrae be not told of my death, or made to grieve on account of me.

'& that I be not bury'd in consecrated ground.

'& that no sexton be asked to toll the bell.

'& that nobody is wished to see my dead body.

'& that no murners walk behind me at my funeral.

'& that no flours be planted on my grave.

'& that no man remember me.

'To this I put my name.

'MICHAEL HENCHARD'.

Why is this document so moving? In what way does it gather up so much of the emotional impact of Henchard? Much of the effect comes from its language: it is stark and direct, using no adjectives, if we except 'consecrated' which is anyway a technical term, not a descriptive or emotive epithet. The recurring and parallel sentences have the effect of a Litany, and the rhythm, partly biblical, partly that of blank verse, gives it a direct emotional impact beyond that of prose, culminating in the marvellous finality of '& that no man remember me.' But it is not style alone that can account for its power; we must consider what Henchard is really saying.

For he is not simply saying that he wants no funeral rites, as Elizabeth-Jane realises when she says 'What bitterness lies there.'

Henchard had last spoken to her at her wedding when she re-proached him so fiercely for deceiving her over Newson:

> Henchard's lips half parted to begin an explanation. But he shut them up like a vice, and uttered not a sound. How should he, there and then, set before her with any effect the palliatives of his great faults ... Among the many hindrances to such a pleading, not the least was this, that he did not suffi-ciently value himself to lessen his sufferings by strenuous appeal or elaborate argument. (Chapter XLIV.)

And so he leaves her, with a speech which clearly anticipates the sentiment of the Will, though without its concentrated bit-terness: 'I'll never trouble 'ee again, Elizabeth-Jane – no, not to my dying day.'

If the world has been cruelly unjust to us, we are usually stung into protest; if in the midst of such protest we are shown that the fault is our own, what happens to our feelings? Indig-nation is no longer possible, but the self-pity is not abolished. We may turn on ourselves with an intensity of self-reproach sharpened by the presence of the self-pity we no longer feel entitled to express. The common form of this response is to say that we wish we were dead – then others would feel sorry for us; they would then feel not the reproach they are entitled to, but the pity to which we are not as entitled as we would wish.

At the end of *Othello*, with Desdemona dead, Iago exposed, and Othello himself arrested and told he will have to answer for his deed, we have one of the most famous death-speeches in tragedy:

> Soft you; a word or two before you go.
> I have done the state some service, and they know't –
> No more of that. I pray you, in your letters,
> When you shall these unlucky deeds relate,
> Speak of me as I am, nothing extenuate,
> Nor set down aught in malice. Then must you speak
> Of one that lov'd not wisely, but too well;
> Of one not easily jealous, but, being wrought,
> Perplexed in the extreme; of one whose hand,
> Like the base Indian, threw a pearl away
> Richer than all his tribe; of one whose subdu'd eyes,

Albeit unused to the melting mood,
Drop tears as fast as the Arabian trees
Their med'cinable gum. Set you down this:
And say besides that in Aleppo once,
Where a malignant and a turbaned Turk
Beat a Venetian and traduced the state,
I took by th' throat the circumcised dog
And smote him – thus.

It is a magnificent *coup de théâtre*: not only the excitement of
the stabbing itself, after the disputes about whether Othello still
had a weapon, but the final glimpse of that dignity and courage
which was so signally Othello's at the beginning of the play,
and from which we saw him so grievously fall. This is the old
Othello back again: the man who stood calm in the middle of
a night brawl with the magnificent line 'Put up your bright
swords, or the dew will rust 'em', quelling violence by the sheer
dignity of his presence – is that not the same man, essentially, as
now says 'When you shall these unlucky deeds relate, Speak
of them as they are', with the dignity of a simple demand for
truth. And here we see confirmed the point made earlier about
tragedy: that a speech like this must be a death speech. After
what has happened to Othello, it would be a mockery for him
to pretend that he is still the man he was; only the pressure of
impending death, the need (and the opportunity) to die well,
can provide the occasion for such a rehabilitation. Tragedy
must end in the death of the hero so that it can end in speeches
like this.

In a famous essay on 'Shakespeare and the Stoicisim of
Seneca' T. S. Eliot treated Othello's dying speech with rather
less respect:

> I have always felt that I have never read a more terrible
> exposure of human weakness – of universal human weak-
> ness – than the last great speech of Othello ... It is usually
> taken at its face value, as expressing the greatness in defeat
> of a noble but erring nature.

He then quotes the speech, and comments:

> What Othello seems to me to be doing in making this speech
> is *cheering himself up*. He is endeavouring to escape reality,

he has ceased to think about Desdemona, and is thinking about himself. Humility is the most difficult of all virtues to achieve; nothing dies harder than the desire to think well of oneself. Othello succeeds in turning himself into a pathetic figure, by adopting an *aesthetic* rather than a moral attitude, dramatizing himself against his environment. He takes in the spectator, but the human motive is primarily to take in himself. I do not believe that any writer has ever exposed this *bovarysme,* the human will to see things as they are not, more clearly than Shakespeare.

This has aroused a good deal of indignation from Shakespearean scholars: to reduce one of the most celebrated of all tragic endings to 'cheering oneself up' is surely to treat tragedy with a kind of lofty disdain, and to turn Shakespeare into a satirist, secretly despising his great hero – and furthermore, to assert that no one had ever noticed the satire until Eliot came along! One can understand the scholars' indignation.

There is a crucial ambiguity about Eliot's comment which we must clear up before we go further. Is he offering us his comment on Shakespeare, or Shakespeare's on Othello – i.e. is he claiming that Shakespeare set out to show this *bovarysme* in his hero? Several details (the last sentence, for instance) suggest that he is, and in that case, surely, the claim is absurd. Hidden messages like this are not signalled secretly across the centuries to waiting critics, like secret codes announcing that the play is really by Francis Bacon. The critic who tells us that Othello is not a tragedy is a crank.

But if we ignore those touches which suggest that Eliot is offering a new reading, and take the passage rather as a comment on Shakespeare – a comment from the outside, as it were – it becomes much more significant – and harder to dismiss. Perhaps Eliot, who clearly feels he is groping his way towards an insight, was uncertain which he was doing; and I suggest that what he was doing was discussing tragedy. Not correcting the traditional reading of *Othello* but accepting it, and then saying, Look what you have been admiring. Even the lofty disdain is not altogether out of place, for the implicitly Christian standpoint of Eliot's criticism can involve a disdain for attempts to come to terms with human situations that do not see it (as tragedy does not) as subordinate to God's plan.

Eliot is claiming that tragedy involves self-pity: that the final gesture of the tragic hero draws its power from the attempt to cut a good figure. Surely there is much truth in this view. We are all familiar with the experience of seeing through ourselves, and the need to regain the dignity we feel ought to be rightfully ours. It is to this need that tragedy appeals. If we can identify ourselves with humanity itself, or at any rate with the tragic hero who seems at that instant to speak for the possibilities in humanity, we shall find the comfort we need, and it will not look merely like comfort.

Is this to despise tragedy? Yes, if our point of view is primarily moral, as Eliot's seems to be when he attributes to Othello an *aesthetic* attitude, a wish to dramatise himself against his environment. But art is by definition an aesthetic not a moral activity. If we are considering the right thing to do, in an actual situation, no doubt it will be unwise to see ourselves as tragic heroes; but if we are expressing an emotional need in memorable form – the need for reassurance that shall seem like self-knowledge (that on one level, though not the deepest, shall be self-knowledge) – then we are not likely to be distracted by being told that we ought to value humility more and heroism less. That colder eye might lead us to Dante instead of Shakespeare, or to preaching instead of poetry.

The point that Eliot found with so much hesitation in *Othello* is surely much clearer in *The Mayor Of Casterbridge*. Henchard is certainly cheering himself up at the end, adopting an aesthetic not a moral attitude, dramatising himself against his environment. His Stoicism has a histrionic quality that nothing but the imminence of death could, after what he has been through, permit. That final document is his curtain speech, and it is the moment at which we identify with him most completely. No doubt a certain kind of austere critic will tell us that it is self indulgent to shed tears for Henchard; but to say that is to prefer virtue to poetry.

4

THE SOCIAL CONTEXT

On 16 November 1910 Hardy received the freedom of the town of Dorchester, an honour that meant more to him than almost any other he was ever given. In his speech of acceptance he remarked that his Casterbridge was not Dorchester – 'not even the Dorchester as it existed sixty years ago, but a dream-place that never was outside an irresponsible book.' Then he continued:

> Nevertheless, when somebody said to me that 'Casterbridge' is a sort of essence of the town as it used to be, 'a place more Dorchester than Dorchester itself', I could not absolutely contradict him, though I could not quite perceive it.[1]

That is as far as we can expect so modest and hesitant a writer to go: Hardy is clearly admitting, despite a kind of wish not to, that his books are about the rural England he knew; and in turning now from the cosmic to the social, from the philosophical and intellectual context to the novels as historically situated in time and place, we are only following where Hardy led. He was as interested in Dorset as in the Universe.

It is first of all necessary to divide the social interpretation of Hardy's novels into two kinds, very different from each other, which we may call the naïve and the sophisticated, or the antiquarian and the sociological. There has always been an interest in the local significance of Hardy's work, as we can see by visiting the Hardy museum in Dorchester, or glancing at the innumerable discussions of the accuracy of his use of dialect, the geography of Wessex, the local customs he inserts into his novels. Hardy himself shared this interest, and the very small body of his writings on literature includes a good deal of local material – prefaces to the works of friends and fellow townsmen, or discussions on how dialect should be represented in novels.

When applied to *The Mayor*, such criticism is likely to concentrate on the two episodes of the wife-sale and the skimmity-ride, for as well as being prominent in the novel they are clearly based on a knowledge of local custom, and assume an interest in this on the part of the reader. In the General Preface to the Wessex Editor of his works (1912), Hardy claimed that he had 'instituted inquiries to correct tricks of memory, and striven against temptations to exaggerate, in order to preserve for my own satisfaction a fairly true record of a vanishing life.'[2] And naturally enough, once he was famous, a host of readers who cared for the vanishing life or the Dorset scene instituted their own inquiries into where Hardy got his details of folk-lore, and followed up all the references to customs and local knowledge. We now know, for instance, not only that there are recorded examples of the sale of wives in the nineteenth century, but also exactly where Hardy got the material for his episode; we know too that Newson paid a good price, for there is a recorded example from Stamford, that Hardy transcribed into his Commonplace Book, in which a fellow sold his wife in a halter for two shillings wet and two shillings dry.[3]

Those interested in comparing Gabriel Oak's weatherlore with popular rustic knowledge on the subject, or Abel Whittle's dialect with how Dorsetmen speak – or spoke; or in knowing how widespread a custom the skimmity-ride was, and that it survived into the twentieth century – those with such matter-of-fact interests in Hardy's rural world will find no shortage of material to consult;[4] but this is not the social context in which I propose to discuss *The Mayor*. I shall leave it alone both through ignorance, and because whatever its interest for one group of readers, it is not there that a quickening context for the novel is to be found today. It is not an antiquarian concern with Hardy's facts that will draw modern readers to his fiction, but a sense of society as a complex and changing world that can be charted and understood – the historian's sense, even the sociologist's. And there has, in the last generation, been a group of critics, most of them influenced by Marxism, who have begun to look at Hardy in just this way, who maintain that his narrative art takes both its material and its vitality from the agricultural, rather than from the philosophical, context',[5] and who therefore prefer to interpret the novels in terms of the historical situation of the author that is, of the agricultural crisis of (approximately) 1870–1900.[6]

This was a time of depression and conflict in English agriculture, when prices fell, under the influence of imported foodstuffs, especially American wheat. Hundreds of thousands of workers left the countryside to look for work in towns; attempts to organise farm workers into a trade union failed, after bitter conflict with the farmers; the amount of land under cultivation fell. England appeared to be paying the full bitter price of the repeal of the Corn Laws, the Free Trade policy that had put industry before agriculture, town before country. The action of *The Mayor*, of course, takes place forty years before it was written: to read it against the contemporary situation, then, could lead us to maintain that it is concerned with the issues of its time, above all with the Corn Law conflict.

It would be an exaggeration to say that there is a sociological school of Hardy critics; for those who use such an approach differ a good deal among themselves in their interpretations. In particular, they often disagree strongly on the nature and strength of the traditional rural community, which some may see as an Arcadia destroyed by capitalist farming methods, and others may consider as much torn by social tensions as what has replaced it. But two important points connect them all. First, they all relate Hardy to social reality, and insist on seeing his novels in relation to the movements actually taking place in nineteenth-century England; and second, they all see Hardy as centrally concerned with social change. Often they will actively object to the sort of criticism that stresses the timeless. Thus Merryn Williams, writing of *Tess*, claims: 'What Fate means is that in her particular social situation it was inevitable that her innocence should be destroyed.'[7] Such a remark is in the main Marxist tradition of literary criticism; for one of the most constant endeavours of Marxist criticism is to show the social basis of what are presented as universal or cosmic questions, and to take what appears to be a conflict between man and his destiny, or between two duties or two drives that are both underwritten by eternal law, and to claim that such conflict is socially determined, usually in terms of class. To such an approach, all timeless categories will have in them an element of evasiveness. 'The absolute,' says Georg Lukacs, 'is nothing but the fixation of thought, it is the projection into myth of the intellectual failure to understand reality concretely as a historical process.'[8] What is seen as existing outside society is not fully understood; the way to find solutions to what appear insoluble dilemmas is to see them as socially determined. Tragedy, by such a view, will appear as an attempt to give the seal of inevitability to a particular conjunction of human relationships.

The social approach to Hardy has many advantages, and has undoubtedly drawn our attention to a good deal that other critics have missed. I do not simply mean by this that it points to the documentary element in the novels, their usefulness as accounts of what was going on in rural England – as amplifications, say, of works like Rider Haggard's *Rural England*, a fierce indictment of the decline of English agriculture. Critics of this school do often use Hardy as a documentor, but at their best they do much more: to see literature in a social perspective makes a number of insights possible.

Let us start with one of the most striking structural features in Hardy – the entrance of a stranger into the community. It is a natural device to anyone constructing a plot, and almost all Jane Austen's novels use it. Darcy and Wickham, Fanny Price, Willoughby, Frank Churchill, Wentworth: the action is often set off by their arrival, and our understanding of the main characters helped by watching their expectations and responses to the newcomer. Everything is slightly rearranged, and a hitherto static situation acquires that element of movement that sets the plot in motion.

That is the formal use of the device; but in Hardy its interest transcends the formal. His strangers do not simply set personal relationships in motion, they represent a new kind of personal relationship, for they come from a world that is foreign to Wessex. This is not true of Jane Austen. By introducing strangers who belong to the culture but do not happen to know that particular community, she concentrates attention on the differences between individuals: this is one reason for saying that the social world of Jane Austen is static. Hardy however, is interested in more than the individuality of his strangers. We can see a development, as his fiction progressed, towards making the stranger more and more alien. Frank Troy, in *Far from the Madding Crowd,* is a local lad who has received (and wasted) more education than the others, and has travelled as a soldier, whereas Alec d'Urberville, in *Tess,* is a townsman who has no connection with Wessex, no right to the ancient name he assumes, and no reverence for the world he tramples on.

The stranger in *The Mayor* is of course Farfrae; and there is no doubt that he brings new ways of thought into Casterbridge. For Farfrae represents economic rationalisation, in contrast to the highly personal way in which Henchard had previously done business. His way of dealing is less dramatic and more reliable, less temperamental and more easily detached from the individual situation:

> Meanwhile, the great corn and hay traffic conducted by Henchard throve under the management of Donald Farfrae as it had never thriven before. It had formerly moved in jolts; now it went on oiled castors. The old crude *vivâ voce* system of Henchard, in which everything depended upon his memory, and bargains were made by the tongue alone, was swept away. Letters and ledgers took the place of 'I'll do't,' and 'you shall hae't,' and, as in all such cases of advance, the rugged picturesqueness of the old method disappeared with its inconveniences. (Chapter XIV.)

This is not merely a digression into social history, it is a summing up of Farfrae's whole behaviour. As a manager we see him treating Abel Whittle with cool good sense instead of Henchard's hot temper; later, as owner, he lowers wages but leaves the private lives of his men alone. He introduces into the agricultural world of Wessex the spirit of the industrial revolution, the depersonalising of labour relations; and so it is not surprising that he introduces the mechanisation of agriculture, by bringing the horse-drill to Casterbridge. Its arrival creates astonishment in the market place: most people are content to wonder, but Henchard ridicules it. He does this because he now hates Farfrae, but underneath the personal dislike we can see a more impersonal reason: Henchard speaks from the rugged and pre-industrial world which he will never be able to step out of, whereas Farfrae is the agent of economic progress, something much larger than him (' "the machines are already very common in the East and North of England," he added apologetically'). Elizabeth-Jane's nostalgic regret that the romance of the sower is gone for good is basically the same kind of rejection of the new as Henchard's impatient scorn.

And it is not merely in economic affairs that Farfrae represents a new world: as man as well as dealer he contrasts with

Henchard. He deals out good will, not in vast all-or-nothing surges, but carefully, steadily and with some degree of calculation. He is willing to go and look for Henchard with his wife, but proposes they return before nightfall so as not to make a hole in a guinea. His courtship of Elizabeth-Jane is based on sober appreciation, not passion. And, most interesting of all, there is his singing. The locals in *The Three Mariners* cannot understand how a man can sing so eloquently about his native land and also be content to leave it, and Hardy, not without a touch of malice, shows him at the wedding singing about 'his dear native country, that he loved so well as never to have re-visited it.' What Farfrae does is to exploit emotion for the purpose of entertainment. He is able to distance himself from it, to *use* it, in a way that parallels his economic activity. Simply because he is not intensely involved, he can handle it competently, as a social grace. His song, like his business, goes on oiled casters.

The social dimension in Elizabeth-Jane's character is less obvious but is also there. What is most striking about her as an individual is her quiet persistence, her dogged attempts at self-improvement, her ability to bear suffering and wait, as she waits for Henchard to appreciate her, or for Farfrae to propose. What is most striking about her socially is her rise: entering Casterbridge as a poor girl who has to help in the waiting at *The Three Mariners* in order to help pay the bill, she finds herself with her own carriage; and then after her setback she rises once again, and becomes the wife of the man who is clearly going to be the richest man in Casterbridge, and will no doubt be Mayor again soon. Now these two aspects of Elizabeth-Jane can be connected. She is the sort of person who rises in the world. In a situation in which social mobility is possible, her quiet persistence is the way to achieve it: her concern with respectability, shown on her very first appearance by her distress at her mother talking to the furmity-woman, is the manifestation of an inner tightness that is quite likely to issue in the achieving of the respectability she models herself on. Her actual rise, of course, is in two stages: her adoption by Henchard near the beginning, and her marriage at the end. The former belongs only to the plot, and has no typical importance; the latter has a wider significance, for the normal way for women to rise in that society was by marriage. Our satisfaction at the happy ending is not merely in her personal good fortune, but at the appropriateness of society having given her fit reward.

The skimmity-ride, as I have already remarked, is a sign of Hardy's interest in tradition; but it also has a social function, since it issues from Mixen Lane. We learn a good deal about the social structure of Casterbridge, as we can see by comparing the three inns – The Kings Arms, where the Mayor's banquet is held; The Three Mariners, the more modest place where ordinary folk sit and drink, and where Farfrae stays on arrival; and Peter's Finger, the 'church' of Mixen Lane, haunt of poachers and good-for-nothings, frequented by Jopp the malcontent. The very names of the inns show the diminishing scale of dignity; and each of the inns is in touch, in its very different way, with the life of the surrounding countryside – by commercial speculation and professional activity; by normal paid labour; and by poaching. Mixen Lane is the home both of lawbreaking and of needy respectability, and it is the part of Casterbridge that receives those driven off the land – copyholders, or those with only insecure tenancies of their cottage, who have found it necessary to migrate to the town. They are early examples of the movement that became so vast in the '70s and '80s, the uprooting of so many thousands of rural labourers, and their drift to the towns – the process that Hardy bitterly described as the tendency of water to flow uphill when forced.[9] We can see that there is nothing idealised about the picture of Casterbridge, and that Hardy is well aware of its underside. What is even more striking is that this underside is so vividly in touch with a past of folk-tradition. A skimmity-ride is clearly thought of by everyone as something old and even old-fashioned: Newson gives money towards it out of something like antiquarian interest. Hardy too, as we have seen, is a kind of antiquarian, but his view of old customs is quite unsentimental: he knows that their links in the present will be with Mixen Lane, and that it is social tensions that keep them alive. It is made clear that envy is the main motive of the skimmity-riders, 'the tempting prospect of putting to the blush people who stand at the head of affairs.' That envy gives vigour to the culture of Mixen Lane emerges in the language too: it is Nance Mockridge, the outspoken enemy of respectability, who shows the

79

most vivid turn of phrase of anyone in the novel, when explaining her pleasure at the thought of what the prank will achieve: 'I do like to see the trimming pulled off such Christmas candles.' The whole episode makes it clear that though Hardy shares the interests of antiquarians, he is much more than an antiquarian himself, for his interest in old customs is not one of uncomprehending nostalgia. He is concerned with the social forces in the present that enable them to stay alive.

We can also, by means of a social approach to the novels, add a gloss to one of the points made in the course of the comparison with Zola. I pointed out then how much more intense is the greed shown by Zola's peasants than anything we find in Hardy, and undoubtedly the main reason for this is the difference in temperament and outlook between the two writers, the savage naturalism of Zola contrasting with the more theoretical pessimism of Hardy. But there is also another reason to be found in the nature of the two societies, and this is the fact that Zola's characters are peasants. In Wessex, those who own the land are not those who work it: English farming had for centuries been on a large scale, using paid labour. The man who spends his days in the fields, helped only by his family, working his own land, for whom questions of inheritance are of crucial importance, is a French not an English figure. Hardy is simply reporting the state of affairs when he gives us prosperous farmers like Boldwood or Crick on the one hand, and wage-earning shepherds or labourers on the other. And it may be that that peculiar hunger for land, that fury of acquisitiveness that translates itself into a fury of work, that peculiar meanness we see in Buteau and old Fouan, is a peasant phenomenon. However, much Zola's vision may have exaggerated it, he too, in a way, is reporting what he sees.

We can add a social comment on Jefferies. Jefferies knows that he lives in a changing world, and one of the most powerful ways to represent social change in a novel is to portray a traditional figure of great strength, and show that he is not able to cope with his situation. Such implicit representation of change can be even more powerful than building it directly into the unfolding of the story, and there is certainly something of this in Iden's increasing indebtedness and his infuriating refusal to adapt. Yet Jefferies does not altogether see Iden as a traditional figure: the interrelation between society and family is more complex and less clear-cut than that. We are told a good deal about Iden's family tree, and we learn that his father was a baker, and that his great-uncle, whom he admires most of all, was a poetry-reader and man of business. In Iden we are seeing a return to the soil, and a not altogether successful one: hence the surprising passage in which Jefferies suggests that he ought to have been an explorer or engineer:

> Here was Iden, with his great brain and wonderful power of observation, who ought to have been a famous traveller in unexplored Africa or Tibet, bringing home rarities and wonders; or, with his singular capacity for construction, a leading engineer, boring Mont Cenis Tunnels and making Panama Canals; or, with his Baconian intellect, forming a new school of philosophy – here was Iden, tending cows, and sitting, as the old story goes, undecidedly on a stile – sitting astride – eternally sitting, and unable to make up his mind to get off on one side or the other. (Chapter IX.)

There is something pathological, in fact, about that absorption in potato-planting, those long regular after-dinner naps: it is the farmer's life as refuge, rather than that of the born farmer. What there is no ambivalence about, however, is Mrs Iden, whose origins are completely urban, and whose bitter discontent with Iden's inability to get off the stile comes from her Flamma inheritance, for she comes of a nervous, radical, intellectual, rather hysterical family. As so often in incompatible marriages, we are seeing a clash between two backgrounds.

But can we do more than collect a few miscellaneous insights into the social implications of Hardy's art? Is it not possible to indicate more generally the nature and limitations of his social concerns as they appear in the novels? To do this will enable us to judge the value and the dangers of a social approach by the critic; more important, it should lead us to understand what the novels are really about.

I begin by pointing out that the agricultural depression of his own time plays little part in Hardy's fiction, and quite clearly none at all in *The Mayor*, which is set forty years earlier. Some critics have claimed that Hardy's awareness of the crisis of agriculture in the 80s sharpened his analysis of the earlier period, and such a claim is of course as impossible to disprove as it is to prove. What makes it unlikely is the complete lack of interest in the great agricultural issue of the time, the repeal of the Corn Laws. It is not even certain whether the action of the book takes place before or after the repeal;[10] and even the opening paragraph of the Preface, which appears to show an awareness of economic forces, has a very different connotation when reflected on:

> Readers of the following story who have not yet arrived at middle age are asked to bear in mind that, in the days recalled by the tale, the home Corn Trade, on which so much of the action turns, had an importance that can hardly be realized by those accustomed to the sixpenny loaf of the present date, and to the present indifference of the public to harvest weather.

What Hardy is here saying is that man's dependence on Nature for his food was more immediate and more obvious then than now. The huge supplies of cheap American grain that came into England and helped to ruin English agriculture (though not, as it happened, until nearly thirty years after the repeal) have had the effect of diminishing this dependence; and this opening paragraph is asking us to forget about such economic changes, and to imagine ourselves in a situation when the relationship to the land was more direct.

What ruins Henchard? It is not economic forces he misjudges, but the weather; the unpredictable element in his business is natural and cyclical, the alternation of good and bad harvests; and the advantage of setting the novel so much earlier in time is to enable us to see the full significance of this. The point should be clear from *The Mayor* alone; but it becomes doubly clear if we revert to the comparison with Zola. Zola, when beginning on his novel, said explicitly that he wanted to show 'where we are going in this agricultural crisis which is so serious at present,' and sure enough, we find in the village of Cloyes an awareness, though groping and distorted, of the importance of agricultural protection. Lequeu, the misanthropic schoolmaster, launches into a long description of the huge plains of American wheat, where the whole of the Beauce would be lost like a tiny plot of land; and his contempt for the rustics who employ him burns through his warnings of what awaits them.

'And you hope to fight all that with your tuppenny tools,' he went on, 'you that know nothing and want nothing: your highest aim is to stay squatting in your old ruts. Heavens, you're already buried knee-deep in the wheat from over there. And the boats will bring more and more of it. Just wait a few years, and you'll be sunk up to your bellies, your shoulders, your mouths – then over your heads! you're up against a river, a torrent, a flood that'll drown you one and all.'

It is an extraordinary passage. We can imagine such eloquence in Hardy, though not in such a torrent; but never, surely, applied to so theoretical a subject, wheatfields no one present has ever seen, significant only because they are an economic threat. The peasants hear and are terrified of 'cette abondance, de ce pain à bon marché qui menaçait le pays'. The irony would have appealed to Hardy, that this image, drawn from the very nature of what they live for, should represent a threat; but Zola's theoretical awareness of the range of economic forces is far beyond the range of his Wessex. It's beyond that of Zola's characters too, as it happens, since they have just elected a Free Trade MP instead of their usual Protectionist, for wholly personal reasons, and without realising what they were doing.

To read through a book like *The Agricultural Revolution* 1750–1880 by Chambers & Mingay with Hardy in mind is to notice how little it has to tell us about the concerns of his novels. The upward and downward movement of prices; the relative prosperity of the labourer in corn growing areas and in pasture; the increase in the size of farms – these are not the issues that appear in Hardy, and underlying economic forces of this kind could never be deduced from his fiction. A simple example is offered by the fair at Weydon Priors. In the first chapter it is large and thriving, and the furmity-woman has a big refreshment tent (though there is already a hint that Weydon is declining; and the furmity-woman's tent is inferior to its neighbour, and spells its notice wrong). When Susan and Elizabeth-Jane come in search of Henchard, nineteen years later, the fair has declined considerably, and the furmity-woman is reduced to a three-legged crock over a wood fire in the open air. Two years later than that the woman is a vagrant, arrested in the streets of Casterbridge, and obviously used to the insides of police-stations; and when Henchard finally revisits the scene after leaving Casterbridge, he goes back to the hill and finds it 'bare of human beings, and almost of aught besides'. Clearly this downward movement is very important to the book. An increasing seediness and dereliction surrounds the circumstances of Henchard's youth and pride, and the decline of fair and furmity-woman corresponds to the decline of Henchard – not just of his fortunes, but even more of his resilience and strength. The individual story is seen in a fitting social setting.

But if we ask what economic forces have brought about this decline, the question is unanswerable. Is the firmity-woman suffering from old age, from the effects of bad character, or from a declining demand for her product? There are enough hints in the first chapter to suggest that her character has much to do with it, but the product is old-fashioned too. We cannot choose between these alternatives, and are not meant to bother. As for the decline of the fair, is it a sign of prosperity or recession? One passing detail – the mention that the new periodical great markets of neighbouring towns were beginning to interfere seriously with the trade carried on here for centuries – suggests that it may be prosperity, though it is still uncertain whether the prosperity of towns means the rise or the fall of the countryside. But once again, we need not ask, for the book will not answer. What matters is the fortunes of the institution, not the underlying economic movements that controlled them. Indeed, if there is any model for what happened to the fair it is not economic but Darwinian: it seems to have lost out in some unexplained struggle for existence.

I have already suggested that the clash between Farfrae and Henchard is that between an old society and a new; now I am claiming that the novel shows little interest in economic forces. How can we find a formula that reconciles these apparently contradictory claims? The answer, I think, is to recognise that Hardy's interest is in life-style. He has the eye of a sociologist, even of an anthropologist, rather than that of an economist. This is very clear in the Henchard-Farfrae contrast – Northern insight matched against Southern doggedness – which can be felt in the way they woo Lucetta, or the way they treat Elizabeth-Jane, as much as in their business dealings. For another example we can look at *Tess*.

> By the engine stood a dark motionless being, a sooty and grimy embodiment of tallness, in a sort of trance, with a heap of coals by his side: it was the engineman. The isolation of his manner and colour lent him the appearance of a creature from Tophet, who had strayed into the pellucid smokelessness of this region of yellow grain and pale soil, with which he had nothing in common, to amaze and to discompose its aborigines.
>
> What he looked he felt. He was in the agricultural world, but not of it. He served fire and smoke; these denizens of the fields served vegetation, weather, frost, and sun. He travelled with his engine from farm to farm, from county to county, for as yet the steam threshing-machine was itinerant in this part of Wessex. He spoke in a strange northern accent; his thoughts being turned inwards upon himself, his eye on his iron charge, hardly perceiving the scenes around him, and caring for them not at all: holding only strictly necessary intercourse with the natives, as if some ancient doom compelled him to wander here against his will in the service of his Plutonic master. The long strap which ran from the driving-wheel of his engine to the red thresher under the rick was the sole tie-line between agriculture and him.
>
> (Chapter XLVII.)

This engineman does not appear again in the story, though the engine does: it is the mechanical threshing machine that wears Tess down while Alec d'Urberville stands below her and tries to win her over, so that she is caught between her two enemies, progress and temptation. The effect of the thresher on those who work in the fields is of enormous concern to Hardy; and the figure of the engineman is that of an invader who represents a threat. The passage does not show Hardy at his best, at any rate in the first paragraph: it falls into the heavy handed elaboration that sometimes overtakes his style ('embodiment of tallness' is indefensible; and 'aborigines' is either pretentious or facetious, and in neither case happy). The opening of the second paragraph, with its brief, blunt sentences, is far more successful, and the contrast of elements is both succinct and successfully traditional; though unfortunately it drops once again into the long-windedness of 'in the service of his Plutonic master.' The final sentence however offers an accurate and striking image of the point being made.

The same situation occurs in a twentieth-century novelist, John Steinbeck's *The Grapes of Wrath*:

> The tractors came over the roads and into the fields, great crawlers moving like insects, having the incredible strength of insects . . . The man sitting in the iron seat did not look like a man: gloved, goggled, rubber dust-mask over nose and mouth, he was a part of the monster, a robot in the seat . . . He could not see the land as it was, he could not smell the land as it smelled: his feet did not stamp the clods or feel the warmth and power of the earth. He sat in an iron seat and stepped on iron pedals. He could not cheer or beat or curse or encourage the extension of his power, and because of this he could not cheer or whip or curse or encourage himself. He did not know or own or trust or beseech the land. If a seed dropped did not germinate, it was nothing. If the young thrusting plant withered in drought or drowned in a flood of rain, it was no more to the driver than to the tractor.

The headlong surge of this prose and the violence of the imagery sound more like Zola than Hardy. It is lurid and overemphatic, and makes Hardy's prose seem timid. There is a journalistic polish to this passage that could neither sink to Hardy's clumsiness nor rise to his delicacy. The point they are making, however, is in both cases the same, and even more so than at first appears. For Steinbeck is quite clear that this brutal method of farming is the way to grow more food: his hostility to it is based on what it does to those working on the land, not on questions of efficiency. And there is nothing in Hardy's account to suggest that the new thresher is anything but efficient: he too is concerned only with the effect of the new methods on those who work the land, contrasting a responsiveness to soil and weather with the isolation of the man who deals with it through a machine. The tractor driver's lunch – 'sandwiches wrapped in waxed paper, white bread, pickle, cheese, Spam, a piece of pie branded like an engine part', that he eats without relish – represents the same isolation as the 'trance' of Hardy's engineman, his reticence and his strange northern accent. Farfrae's Scottish speech was odd but amusing, but by the time of *Tess* Hardy has grown more worried at the invaders.

We have two documents written by Hardy which record his views on the agricultural history of his time, an essay *The Dorsetshire Labourer,* written in 1884, and a letter to Rider Haggard, who was collecting material for his *Rural England.* Both of them are surprisingly optimistic on economic questions. The *Dorsetshire Labourer* speaks of the advantages to the labourers of their comparative economic independence, and of the habit of shifting around from one workplace to another: 'they have become shrewder and sharper men of the world, and have learnt to hold their own with firmness and judgement.' The letter to Rider Haggard describes the poverty and hardship of agricultural labourers down to the middle of the nineteenth century, and goes on to say that things are widely different now. 'Their present life is almost without exception one of comfort, if the most ordinary thrift be observed.' There is even a surprisingly radical political comment in the essay, to the effect that 'if a farmer can afford to pay 30 per cent more wages in times of agricultural depression than he paid in times of agricultural prosperity . . . the labourer must have been greatly wronged in those prosperous times.' This is the side of Hardy's social interests that does not appear in the novels, and it shows a straightforward satisfaction at material progress. But neither of these essays is an altogether optimistic document, for when the changes in rural life are looked at as a whole, they are seen to have undermined much of what was most valuable in traditional culture. The very change that has given the labourers a new independence – the fact that they are able and willing to change employer so frequently – has been one of the most ruinous of all.

> I cannot recall a single instance of a labourer who still lives on the farm where he was born, and I can only recall a few who have been five years on their present farms. Thus you see, there being no continuity of environment in their lives, there is no continuity of information, the names, stories, and relics

of one place being speedily forgotten under the incoming facts of the next. For example, if you ask one of the workfolk (they always used to be called 'workfolk' hereabouts – 'labourers' is an imported word) the names of surrounding hills, streams; the character and circumstances of people buried in particular graves; at what spots parish personages lie interred; questions on local fairies, ghosts, herbs, etc., they can give no answer.

This is a point Hardy had already made in the Preface to *Far From the Madding Crowd*, in which he describes a number of old customs that were thriving at the time the story is set and have since disappeared, and concludes that the reason for this is 'the recent supplanting of the class of stationary cottagers . . . by a population of more or less migratory labourers.' The result of this is to destroy legend, folk-lore, close inter-social relations, and eccentric individualities. 'For these the indispensable conditions of existence are attachment to the soil of one particular spot by generation after generation.' *Far from the Madding Crowd* itself does not record the change; the Preface merely sets down Hardy's observation that the word it does record has begun to pass away; and perhaps also his realisation that the loving understanding with which he recreates it is based on an awareness that it is passing.

The connection between material improvement and cultural loss is one Hardy was well aware of; and it is not of course new to him. Perhaps the best parallel in the nineteenth century novel is provided by Scott, whose novels depict a violent, colourful, even fanatical way of life that is contrasted implicitly – sometimes even explicitly – with the reasonable world inhabited by author and reader. Scott's rather neutral heroes, sensible young men with a career to make, find themselves having to choose between rebellion and the status quo in a way that also involves a choice between adventure and responsibility, enthusiasm and balance; and to ask which side Scott prefers, and which side he wishes us to choose, is to reduce the splendid objectivity of his work to the level of a crude moral choice.

Hardy believed that tremendous cultural upheaval was taking place in rural England. There had been an old way of life, characterised by the slow rhythms of agricultural work, fixed social relationships, the colourful speech of dialect, manual skills passed on through the generations, legends and folk tales and superstitions. It was going out before a new way that involved rationalised work processes, calculation instead of impulse, lower toleration of eccentricity, and influence from the towns penetrating the countryside. As a man, he was no more able to take sides in this contrast than Scott was. 'It is the old story,' he wrote in The *Dorsetshire Labourer,* 'that progress and picturesqueness do not harmonise.' But as a novelist, he displayed so deep a loyalty to the old that his books have been read as a celebration of it. Yet the sense of change is never absent. In *Far From the Madding Crowd* it is diffused, and its function is mainly to sharpen the perceptiveness with which the old way is apprehended; as his writing progressed, the change more and more entered the action of the book, until in *Jude* the modern world itself provides the setting, with a sense informing it that an older world has been left behind. As he developed, too, he took an increasingly gloomy view of the change, showing less and less trust in the ability of the old to resist degradation. But the gloom is caused by the cultural change, and is quite compatible with believing that it had brought economic improvement. What has passed is a way of life.

If we could find a terminology to describe the change, it would enable us to fit Hardy's outlook into a theoretical framework; and I suggest that we find a pair of concepts that fit it well, in the work of the German sociologist Tönnies. Tönnies analyses society in terms of the contrast between Gemeinschaft (community) and Gesellschaft (company or association).[11] It is both a contrast between different stages of historical development, and between antithetical categories in a static state. Gemeinschaft draws on the fact that man is a social being; it is a grouping in which Wesenwille (natural or integral will) predominates, and men belong to it by a direct emotional bond; it involves relationships between strong and weak seen as organic and natural. The Gemeinschaft may be held together by blood (kinship) or by place (neighbourhood or village) or by mind (friendship); the folkways in which it issues do not need explicit rules for their enforcement. In the Gesellschaft, on the other hand, human beings are essentially separated: a condition of tension between members is assumed as the norm. The Gesell-schaft is based essentially on the act of exchange: it is funda-mentally an economic association, and the process of giving exchange value to different goods is the content of the social will that holds it together. On this economic association, political institutions and scientific thought can be superimposed, for the isolating processes of reason have now come into being.

Traditional rural society, as seen by Hardy, is surely a Gemeinschaft. Everyone belongs to it in a completely unques-tioning way, from birth: no conscious decision is needed to join, and an outsider would not normally be thought to belong. It is a hierarchical society that accepts unquestioningly the relations between strong and weak as institutionalised in property. Kin-ship and locality are the two dominant modes of association, for most people the only two. The change that comes over this world, the change to modernism progress and discontent, is the advent of the Gesellschaft.

This can be seen most clearly if we contrast *Far From the Madding Crowd* and *Jude the Obscure*. The farm labourers of the earlier novel do not question or even understand the bonds that hold them together: work-relationships and human re-lationships are inseparable. The isolating processes of abstract reasoning mean nothing to those in this society, as we can see from Jan Coggan's opinions on religion:

'Chapel-folk be more hand-in-glove with them above than we', said Joseph, thoughtfully.
'Yes,' said Coggan. 'We know very well that if anybody do go to heaven, they will. They've worked hard for it, and they deserve to have it, such as 'tis. I bain't such a fool as to pre-tend that we who stick to the Church have the same chance as they, because we know we have not. But I hate a feller who'll change his old doctrines for the sake of getting to heaven. I'd as soon turn king's-evidence for the few pounds you get. Why, neighbours, when every one of my taties were frosted, our Pa'son Thirdly were the man who gave me a sack for seed, though he hardly had one for his own use, and no money to buy 'em. If it hadn't been for him, I shouldn't hae had a tatie to put in my garden. D'ye think I'd turn after that? (Chapter **XLII**.)

Are we meant to laugh at Coggan? Well of course, put into the theological language he uses, the point is absurd: nothing (to a Christian) takes precedence over salvation. Yet Coggan's naïvety is wiser than the theologian's logic, for he puts community before dogma. He values church doctrine because he values the social function of the parson, and because it is 'old ancient doctrine', integrated into his way of life; he does not fully understand it, and it is less use to him in personal emotional crises than evangelical theology would be to chapel-folk, but his need is for what ties him to his unquestioned way of life.

In contrast to this, the life of Jude Fawley is all restlessness. In this last novel, Hardy left the rural community, and wrote about the quest for education, advancement and sexual fulfilment in the modern urban world. Jude and Sue have no old ancient doctrines to fall back on, for their needs are new, and they need to construct their creeds by means of the Kürwille – the rational will which distinguishes ends and means, contrasted by Tönnies with the Wesenwille. Hardy's attitude to the new world of Gesellschaft in *Jude the Obscure* is deeply ambivalent. On the one hand, he sympathises completely with Jude's struggle for education, and resents the bigotry of a university that can offer no response to his aspirations; just as he admires Phillotson for flouting convention and allowing Sue to leave him when their marriage has become a hollow union, thus setting a new emancipated code above all ancient doctrine. Tradition appears frequently as narrow, oppressive and cold. But on the other hand, the novel suggests that the restless aspirations of Jude, and even more of Sue, are somehow diseased, that they represent the ache of modernism, a loss of the traditional values of rural life, that appear only peripherally in this book in the person of widow Edlin.

It is impossible to say clearly which side Hardy is on; and even in *Far From the Madding Crowd* Joseph Poorgrass and Jan Coggan are somehow morally stunted. They are holding this very conversation in the tavern, at a time when Joseph ought to be taking a coffin to the churchyard, and by neglecting the duty he inadvertently causes great distress to his mistress. Traditional society lacks moral imagination in a crisis.

Hardy is not, in the end, as ambivalent as Scott, but it is none the less impossible to read his fiction as a clear preference for the old over the new. It was for this reason that I refused, in the Introduction, to use 'moral' as one of the terms to describe the 'impure' approach to literature: for morality implies preference, and in the finest works of literature preference may not be easy. And even if it is clear that Hardy does often prefer the Gemeinschaft, it would be wrong to claim that the value of the work lies there. Nostalgia may have provided much of the incentive to write about the contrast, as it fairly clearly does with Tönnies as well; but what we value is the clear awareness of what each kind of world is like. Literature is not simply an opportunity for moral choice, but an exploration of the nature of the alternatives, and Hardy's greatness lies not in his preference but in his full rendering of the life of Gemeinschaft, warts and all.

Perhaps there is no novel that does this as well as *The Mayor*. The contrast between Henchard and Farfrae is that between the man of Gemeinschaft and the man of Gesellschaft. Of course Henchard is not a representative man – there was no one else in Casterbridge like him; just as Gabriel Oak was not a typical shepherd – Bathsheba was lucky to get him. But Oak is representative in the sense that he is the community's best self, as others intuitively recognise; and Henchard is representative in the sense that his rugged individuality shows an incapacity for smooth abstraction altogether characteristic of the old culture – he is the kind of exceptional man it produced.

The society depicted in *The Mayor* corresponds closely to the urban stage of Gemeinschaft as described by Tönnies, in which the exchange of goods between town and country has developed.

In this relationship the country enjoys the obvious advantage which rests with the possession of necessary as compared with more dispensable goods, unless it needs tools and other implements of farming. The town has the advantage of producing rare and beautiful goods, whereby it is assumed that in a large rural area only a select group of its population is concentrated in the town, and therefore the number of workers who produce surplus grains and meat are in the ratio of two to one to those who make objects of handicraft and art for purposes of exchange. It is, by the way, assumed that none of these is a professional trader who, in competition with others, tries his hardest to sell his goods, or that any of them is a monopolist who waits for the need of his customers to become more urgent and their offers in consequence more favourable in order to obtain the highest possible price. There are no doubt such possibilities, but they will materialize only to the degree that nonworking middlemen take hold of things.

If 'nonworking' means that they do not in the narrow sense produce wealth, then both Henchard and Farfrae are such middlemen; and the personal rivalry between them has intensified Henchard's efforts to compete, and to obtain the highest possible price. Casteridge, we see, is poised on the edge of the next phase of economic development in which trade takes on sufficient of an independent life to produce a trading class. Tönnies' analysis helps us to formulate our impression that Henchard has begun something which Farfrae will continue.

The striking difference between economic competitiveness in the two men is that it is so much more personal in Henchard. He concentrated so furiously on buying and selling for maximum gain in an effort to break his rival; whereas Farfrae, as we see from his speech to Lucetta already quoted, is exercising a skill: he wants to succeed in competition for the sake of the success itself, and is quite uninterested in the identity of his commercial opponent. Henchard practises some of the new methods by accident, as it were; Farfrae is to the manner born.

* * *

The change from Gemeinschaft to Gesellschaft is the replacing of one social order by another: it is not simply part of a continuous and ongoing process, but a qualitative change, a single cultural upheaval. To see Hardy's world in this way, then, is to emphasise the completeness of the cultural break, and to see the old world as shocked by it, rather than as already preparing for it, even responsible for it. Is this the right way to view the traditional world of Wessex?

Several diary entries, reprinted in Florence Emily Hardy's *Life*, are suggestive here. In 1887 we find him writing:

It is the on-going – i.e. the 'becoming – of the world that produces its sadness. If the world stood still at a felicitous moment there would be no sadness in it.[13]

This suggests that a static state is Hardy's idea of felicity, and change itself is distressing. Did he consider that the culture of Wessex, before the impact of modernism, was in that state? An entry for 1890 suggests that he did. Speculating why the superstitions of a remote Asiatic and a Dorset labourer are the same, he notes the 'excellently neat' answer of Mr Clodd, that:

The attitude of man at corresponding levels of culture, before like phenomena, is pretty much the same, your Dorset peasants representing the persistence of the barbaric idea.[14]

Hardy goes on of course to defend this idea against any pejorative implications of the word 'barbaric'; what concerns us here is his evident belief that the culture of the Dorset labourer is the same as the very much older barbaric culture of Asia. It clearly implies a view of the farmer as not having changed for hundreds, perhaps thousands, of years, until the impact of modernism; and so suggests that it is that static state which can in certain lyrical moods be seen as felicity.

Now precisely this view of Hardy has recently been attacked as underestimating the realism and complexity of his view: most notably by Raymond Williams, who makes out so clear and perceptive a case that I shall pause to consider it before proceeding. Williams claims that the true way to see the Wessex novels is to recognise that the old society was already changing, and that the tensions in the novels are produced as much by pressures from within that society as by those impinging from outside. Now in an obvious sense this is clearly correct. If the old society had had no tensions it could have produced no stories, and the rich ballad heritage and the handing down of folk-tales, so valued by Hardy, and so often found embedded in his work by old-fashioned critics, would never have come into being. For these tales are not merely stories of individual quirkiness, they are based in the understanding of a culture. But Williams' point is more far-reaching than this: by emphasising the class-divisions in rural society he directs our attention to much that we might otherwise miss. The seduction of Tess, for instance, cannot simply be seen as the rape of the old culture by the urban invader for Tess had begun to emerge from her mother's easy-going world before Alex d'Urberville arrived: she had passed the sixth standard in the National School, and there had been question that she should herself become a teacher, in which case she might have been like Fancy Day, in *Under the Greenwood Tree,* able to go up or down in the social scale according to whom she married. Marriage, as Williams points out, has long been the way of rising socially, especially for women; so that there had always been an element of mobility, just as rural society had always had some sort of contact with the world outside (in the midst of the idyllic Phase Three of *Tess,* the happy summer at the Talbothays Dairy Farm, we are reminded that the milk is sent to London by train every evening). Williams also points to a shrewd and interesting discussion in *The Return of the Native* of the relation between social advancement and intellectual interests, in which Clym is shown to be unrealistic in expecting the rustics, whom he hopes to educate, to seek the latter without looking for the former first. Williams comments, with justice:

> This is not country against town, or even in any simple way custom against conscious intelligence. It is the more complicated and more urgent historical process in which education is tied to social advancement within a class society.[15]

There is, I am sure, an ideological purpose behind this interpretation. I have already suggested that socially oriented critics are likely to resist 'timeless' interpretations, and have shown the basis of this in Marxist thought. Raymond Williams has been strongly influenced by Marxism, though he is too individual a thinker to be adequately described by any label; and even this modified timelessness clearly seems to him an overidealistic reading of Hardy.

The issue is a complex one, and what Williams finds is often really there; all the same, I think his emphasis is wrong, and that there is far more truth in the more familiar reading of Hardy, which sees him as recording the advent of change in a world hitherto hardly touched by historical movements, than there is in his. Many of Williams' examples (and all the more crucial ones) are taken from the later novels; for the general darkening of Hardy's view as the Wessex novels progressed fed back into his version of traditional society.[16] But many of his examples, too, concern economic questions ('it is not urbanism but the hazard of small-capital farming that changes Gabriel Oak from an independent farmer to a hired labourer'), and I have already claimed that this is not the area Hardy is centrally concerned with. Social and economic upsets in a society will eventually (to a materialist) mean cultural strain, but their appearance (usually not very centrally) in a novel need not undermine the apparent permanence of the way of life there depicted – especially if they seem cyclic or unpredictable, the sort of upset that the countryman's philosophy has learnt to treat with Stoicism or resignation.

Turning to illustrations, I look first at a very specific area of the culture: its language. The great upheaval here is the imposition of Standard English on the local dialect, a process Hardy was most interested in. Introducing the poems of the Dorset poet William Barnes, who wrote in dialect, Hardy described how education had 'gone on with its silent and inevitable effacements, reducing the speech of this country to uniformity, and obliterating every year many a fine old local word.'[17] There is no suggestion here that the dialect too was developing speech: the arrival of Standard English is seen as the replacement of one language by another, a single great change, not an extension of already existing change.

The question of dialect crops up in *The Mayor* in the form of Henchard's irritation with Elizabeth-Jane, where her use of local words, along with her democratic way of treating the maid and her having waited at the *Three Mariners,* are seen as examples of her commonness. We are given examples of dialect words – 'dumbledores' for bumble bees, 'walking together' for being engaged – more or less without comment, but their greater vividness and concreteness is obvious, most of all in the last example ('hag-rid' for 'suffering from indigestion'). The function of this detail in the story is doubly ironic. It is Henchard, representative of the old world, who objects to dialect, because (like Melbury in *The Woodlanders*) he wants to feel that his daughter has reached a higher level socially than himself: this is certainly an example of a movement from within traditional society. But the touching reversal at the end puts Henchard back where he belongs: when he is leaving Casterbridge he calls her Izzy, and it sounds like his true speech.

How much history do Hardy's novels contain? They are aware of contemporary change, and one of them, *The Trumpet-Major*, is set during the Napoleonic Wars, the one great historical event that haunted Hardy's imagination, and on which he eventually wrote his epic-drama *The Dynasts*. The significance of the wars was cosmic as much as social for Hardy, and it is not at all clear that he saw this great upheaval as having changed English society in any way. For in Hardy's picture of English history, there is little that changes society. The agriculture of nineteenth-century Dorset was not a system that had existed from time immemorial: it was the result of the growth of capitalist farming and scientific methods. The improvement in winter feeds, that made it unnecessary to slaughter cattle in the autumn, and the enclosure movement from the sixteenth to the eighteenth centuries – these are the influences that shaped and transformed English agriculture. But there is no enclosure movement in Hardy, and little sense that the farming methods and social relationships of Wessex are themselves the product of property relationships and accumulating experience that have changed over the centuries.

It is not that Hardy lacks a historical sense; but if we had to describe this sense, I suggest we should call it archeological. In an interview he gave on Stonehenge in 1899, he confessed to liking 'the state of dim conjecture in which we stand with regard to its history',[18] and in the strange, melodramatic yet moving scene at the end of *Tess*, when Tess is arrested at Stonehenge, the heathen temple exists as if in a state of dim conjecture. They stumble on it in the dark, and its function in the story depends on uncertainty not knowledge, uncertainty of its age, its meaning, its original purpose.

History in *The Mayor* is represented by the Romans whose presence in – or rather under – Casterbridge is powerfully hinted at.

> Casterbridge announced old Rome in every street, alley and precinct. It looked Roman, bespoke the art of Rome, concealed dead men of Rome. It was impossible to dig more than a foot or two deep about the town fields and gardens without

coming upon some tall soldier or other of the Empire, who had lain there in his silent unobtrusive rest for a space of fifteen hundred years. (Chapter XI.)

The sense of the past here is of a past which exists in layers. The past is present not in the form of social forces or institutions, but as material remains that lend a sense of long antiquity to the local scene; its function is emotional and apparent, not invisible and detectable only by sociological analysis. The Amphitheatre, or Ring as it is called (there is no need, when the past has this kind of existence, to call things by their correct names), is used by Casterbridge folk only for furtive appointments, not for those of happy lovers. The only explanation Hardy offers – that its associations had about them something sinister – is almost tautological. The history of the Amphitheatre is given in terms of a series of memorable events – hangings and burnings – that could have taken place at any time and in any order. It is tempting to say that what we have here is a sense of the past – vivid, grotesque, compelling – but not a sense of history.

Wessex then is rich with an unchanging past. Hardy himself sums it up in *Far From the Madding Crowd*:

In these Wessex nooks the busy outsider's ancient times are only old; his old times are still new; his present is futurity.
(Chapter XXII.)

The difference between a static and dynamic society is not absolute: this suggestion that change moved very slowly in Wessex amounts to saying that it was experienced as stasis. The last clause, of course, can be read as a threat if the outsider represents (as, being 'busy' he perhaps does) the accelerated change of the urban world; but as far as the past is concerned, the casual turning up of buried Roman skeletons in the back garden is the perfect example of ancient times being only old.

I have tried to give particular examples for my reading of the novels, but in the end I have to say that it rests on an overwhelming impression. The impact of the world of Troy and Wildeve, Fitzpiers and Farfrae, Angel Clare and Alex d'Urberville, is shattering, and is different in kind from any of the strains and tensions already in the society. This difference can be felt in the nature of the plots. There are crises and adventures that belong in the traditional world, and that it has learnt to contain; and there is the feeling of a new kind of threat, even a new kind of consciousness, that issues in something in the flavour of the book which is easy to sense though almost impossible to define. Bathsheba's joke with the Valentine, that has such a violent and eventually tragic impact on Boldwood, is exactly the sort of crisis that could always have occurred – the impulsive prank of an irresponsible young girl, exercised in a traditional framework, and the consequences, however terrible, will be worked out within their framework. This is not quite so true of her entanglement with Troy: something seems there to have come in from outside and seized her. The difference is slight in *Far From the Madding Crowd*, but more marked in *The Mayor*. Susan's trick over Elizabeth-Jane's identity, like Henchard's sale of his wife, is the stuff of ballads or of the stories the Wessex locals had always told one another. When the two outsiders, Lucetta and Farfrae, are involved, we have a clash of consciousnesses, a constrast between life-styles, that produces a situation in which the contending parties may not fully understand each other. These may not be the most violent or tragic stories, but they are the ones with the widest social significance.

5

CONCLUSION

I have tried to look at *The Mayor of Casterbridge* in two contrasting contexts. On the one hand, that of Hardy's philosophy (which in its turn can be placed in the context of nineteenth-century agnostic and pessimistic thought): that led us to a consideration of tragedy, and to seeing the novel as a statement about man's timeless condition. And on the other, that of rural England on the edge of a social revolution, and of one part of rural England in particular – Dorset, where Hardy grew up and which he knew so intimately. I hope I have managed to show that each of these approaches throws a good deal of light on the novel.

Which is the right context, and the right approach? I hope I have shown too that this is not a useful question. Men belong to their age and to all time: their actions and their character are determined both by particular social circumstances and also by larger and more unchanging factors, and a work of literature, which is a statement about the human condition, will have both particular and universal dimensions. Which you prefer to study may depend partly on what authors you are studying (Hardy is particularly suitable to both approaches) and partly on what kind of critic you are. This essay has been written with a pluralist assumption, that it is not necessary to make this choice. For more important than whether a critic is concerned with the universal or the social, is how far his awareness of the one implies an awareness of the other. When treating *The Mayor* as tragedy, or as cosmic statement, we ought not to lose sight of the actuality of Casterbridge, the marvellous matter-of-factness, the eye for practical detail. If the Spirit Ironic is at work, she is not seated on high in a realm of impersonal Destinies, but she dresses like Dorset folk and speaks in a Dorsetshire accent. When treating it as a social novel, we ought not to shut our ears to the way it is like Shakespeare, to the timeless grandeur of Henchard, and to the fact that it offers constant parallels, structural and emotional, to very different works about very different societies.

But to conclude I want to suggest that these two approaches to Hardy do not conflict quite as much as one might assume; if we are to find one unified way of describing his fiction it will be to see that he is a Dorset Aeschylus, a provincial scholar, a man who sees the universal with local eyes. To say this is not just to join words together, but to point to something central in the final impact of his novels.

Unfortunately, those who have seen him this way have usually intended it as a hostile judgement: calling him a bucolic Schopenhauer is not a compliment. It suggests someone whose learning is home-made, acquired too earnestly and produced too eagerly. Henry James, that most sophisticated of novelists, was very patronising to Hardy, from the time he reviewed *Far From the Madding Crowd* in 1874, and wrote 'Everything human in the book strikes us as factitious and insubstantial; the only things we believe in are the sheep and the dogs',[1] until he wrote in 1892 'The good little Thomas Hardy has scored a great success with *Tess of the d'Urbervilles*, which is chock-full of faults and falsity and yet has a singular beauty and charm.'[2] It is understandable that admirers of Hardy, in reaction against this, should insist on his intelligence and genuine learning, should see the influence of Vergil on his poetry and a subtle awareness of social complexities, or even economic history, in his fiction.[3]

If calling Hardy a Dorset Aeschylus means that he should have left Greek tragedy or philosophy alone, and stuck to his simple ballad stories, then it is a view which degrades him. But it need not mean that: it can be a way of saying that he has his own way of finding tragic situations in ballad material, or of attaching pessimistic reflections to country stories, just as he has his own personal style that is best when it does not deny its eccentricity. Perhaps the point is best illustrated on the level of style, and I have therefore chosen a particular passage to end on – not from *The Mayor of Casterbridge*, whose language is so much more chastened and functional than many of the other novels, but from *The Return of the Native*. It is the description of Clym Yeobright towards the end of the novel:

His sorrows had made some change in his outward appearance; and yet the alteration was chiefly within. It might have been said that he had a wrinkled mind. He had no enemies, and he could get nobody to reproach him, which was why he so bitterly reproached himself.

He did sometimes think he had been ill-used by fortune, so far as to say that to be born is a palpable dilemma, and that instead of men aiming to advance in life with glory they should calculate how much to retreat out of it without shame. But that he and his had been sarcastically and pitilessly handled in having such irons thrust into their souls he did not maintain long. It is usually so, except with the sternest of men. Human beings, in their generous endeavour to construct a hypothesis that shall not degrade a First Cause, have always hesitated to conceive a dominant power of lower moral quality than their own; and, even while they sit down and weep by the waters of Babylon, invent excuses for the oppression which prompts their tears.

He frequently walked the heath alone, when the past seized upon him with its shadowy hand, and held him there to listen to its tale. His imagination would then people the spot with its ancient inhabitants: forgotten Celtic tribes trod their tracks about him, and he could almost live among them, look in their faces, and see them standing beside the barrows which swelled around, untouched and perfect as at the time of their erection. Those of the dyed barbarians who had chosen the cultivable tracts were, in comparison with those who had left their marks here, as writers on paper beside writers on parchment. Their records had perished long ago by the plough, while the works of these remained. Yet they all had lived and died unconscious of the different fates awaiting their works. It reminded him that unforeseen factors operate in the production of immortality.

The Return of the Native is a remarkable book. Of all Hardy's major novels, it is probably the most melodramatic and the most flawed; yet at the same time it is the one most imbued with his quirky sensibility and his feeling for local custom and for landscape. Lovers of Hardy sometimes rate it highest among his works; those who like Hardy best when he is most like other great novelists usually think little of it. It is certainly the book to look at in order to find his prose at its most characteristic.

In this passage, the juxtaposition of Dorset Hardy and Hardy the scholar is very striking. The local interest is most prominent in the final paragraph, with its air of unpretentious antiquarian knowledge; it sounds well-informed, like something by a member of the local archeological society. The unconventional simile in which it culminates ('as writers on paper beside writers on parchment') comes from the mental furniture of just such a man, and helps to preserve a unity of tone. Then, in the rest of the paragraph, we see the limitations of such an outlook: the conclusion which Clym draws is not worthy of the observation: the feel of a man genuinely noticing what is interesting about a landscape which he sees in depth culminates in a trivial remark empty of all intellectual interest.

In the second paragraph the knowledge we are being shown is not local but central: the references are to Greek tragedy and the Bible, and they are made with unusual restraint. Hardy's literary and mythological references are often explicit and sometimes seem dragged in, as if to show off his learning, but in this case he has not drawn our attention to the source of Clym's remark, which is a close paraphrase of what is said by more than one Greek tragic chorus. It is not even clear whether Clym is conscious of the allusion, or whether Hardy wants us to feel that he came independently to the conclusion.

And having come to the conclusion, he does not stay in it: for he is human enough to 'invent excuses for the oppression'. Here we are in the presence of the nineteenth-century agnostic, for whom the whole history of religious thought is a series of errors. There is a strong suggestion here that the King-of-Dahomey view is right, and that man's reluctance to admit it is something between imperceptiveness and generosity. 'Generous' is a brilliant touch: without abandoning his condescending superiority to those who can accept belief in a benevolent Deity, he manages to suggest that their delusion has a moral grandeur – they are better than the God who controls them. It is a highly eccentric religious comment, very similar to that which underlies the poem 'God's Education'.

This paragraph has an eccentric, even laboured brilliance: on top of Clym's impressive but somehow expected reflections comes Hardy's quirky comment. The short first paragraph of the passage, however, has a brilliance that draws no attention to itself. A straightforward opening sentence, that is recapitulated in the marvellous image of the second; then back to a plain style for the psychological insight of the last.

Here is a writer who is always interesting and sometimes brilliant: who imposes his own sensibility on whatever he has to say. This is the prose of *The Return of the Native* at its best, free from the clumsy learning, and the pretentiousness, that have led so many to call Hardy provincial. Yet I have tried to suggest that this passage is provincial too – in the third paragraph, in the sense of a man reworking orthodox thought to fit his own concerns, and in one striking detail in the second paragraph which I have not yet mentioned – 'in having such irons thrust into their souls.' The eighteenth verse of the 104th psalm, which the Authorised Version correctly translates 'Whose feet they hurt with fetters; he was laid in iron', is rendered in most of the other early Bible translations, 'the iron entered into his soul.' The mistake comes from the Latin version, which muddled up the Hebrew original (literally it says 'his soul came into iron'), but this mistranslation has become an English proverb, to express the bitterness brought about by long captivity or oppression. Hardy has altered the proverb, and it is hard to be sure whether he is showing ignorance, or learning, or originality. Is he simply misremembering the famous phrase? Or is he aware that it is normally misused, and by putting 'irons' into the plural (meaning, of course, 'fetters') reminding us of the correct Authorised Version rendering? That will not quite do, however: for the verb 'thrust' does not suggest fetters but swords (an archaic meaning of 'irons'). What we have is someone reworking a famous text for his own purposes, and not afraid to treat it in cavalier fashion.

In one of the best essays ever written on Hardy, his friend Edmund Gosse protested against the 'jarring note of rebellion' that he saw growing in him in *Tess* and *Jude*. 'What has Providence done to Mr Hardy' he wrote, 'that he should rise up in the arable land of Wessex and shake his fist at his Creator?'[4] It is a marvellously perceptive remark. The tone of sophisticated condescension may at first offend an admirer of Hardy; though on reflection it seems clear to me that Gosse admires and envies what he claims to be condescending to (and the rest of the review confirms this). Gosse is obviously aware of the element of perversity in Hardy's pessimism that Empson was complaining of, though he sees its tremendous theatricality at the same time. He is aware too of the clumsiness that Henry James was so sensitive to, but the clumsiness is impressive at the same time. He is even aware that Wessex is not a setting of untouched nature but a community of food-growers. It is a sentence whose resonant grotesqueness must surely have delighted Hardy himself.

Every writer creates his own blend of tradition and individual talent, acclimatising images and themes that have come down to him in his own highly personal world. Few however can be seen to bridge so large and so prominent a gap as Hardy does. I see no reason for apology in this quality of Hardy's: the uniqueness of his art lies in his ability to travel so far from Wessex in his reading, to bring so much home, and to plant it there. His agnosticism, his awareness of intellectual change, his response to Greek tragedy, are always intelligent, always genuine; but in writing them down he never forgets who he is. He has the strength but not the weakness of the self-taught. He is the successful scholarship boy who feels no temptation to despise his parents.

NOTES

Chapter 1. Text
  1. F. E. Hardy, *The Life of Thomas Hardy*, London 1962. p. 176.
  2 *ibid* p. 179.

Chapter 2. The Literary Context
  1 *The Review of Reviews*, February, 1892. See Lerner and Holmstrom, *Thomas Hardy and his Readers*, p. 75.
  2 Jeanette L. Gilder in *The World*, 13 November, 1895. *See ibid.* p. 113.
  3 F. E. Hardy p. 116.
  4 This point is well made in Tony Tanner, 'Colour and Movement in Hardy's *Tess of the D'Urbervilles*'; *Critical Quarterly* (1968) Vol. X p. 219ff.

Chapter 3. The Philosophical Context
  1 F. E. Hardy p. 153.
  2 *ibid.* p. 205.
  3 *ibid.* p. 111.
  4 *ibid.* p. 405.
  5 *ibid.* p. 179.
  6 *ibid.* p. 332.
  7 *ibid.* p. 139.
  8 *ibid.* p. 376.
  9 *ibid.* p. 415.
 10 *ibid.* p. 332.
 11 *ibid.* p. 224.
 12 See also the letter from T. H. to Florence Henniker 11 June 1914. *One Rare Fair Woman* (T. H.'s letters to Florence Henniker) ed. Hardy and Pillion, London 197, p. 161.
 13 F. E. Hardy, p. 407ff.
 14 *The Spectator*, 23 January, 1892. See Lerner and Holmstrom, *Thomas Hardy and his Readers*, p. 69.
 15 F. E. Hardy, p. 243.
 16 William Empson, *The Structure of Complex Words*, London 1951, p. 154.
 17 F. E. Hardy p. 218.
 18 R. H. Hutton in *The Spectator* 5 June 1886. See Lerner and Holmstrom, *Thomas Hardy and his Readers*, p. 53.
 19 Hardy's revisions of *The Mayor* are described in Mary Ellen Chase T. H. from Serial to Novel, NY1964, ch. 2. and (more fully) in Dieter Riesner, 'Kunstprosa in der Werkstatt', *Festschrift fur Walter Hubm*, Berlin 1964.
 20 R. B. Heilman, *Tragedy and Melodrama: Versions of Experience*, Seattle 1968 p. 28.
 21 *ibid.* p. 20.
 22 Roy Morrell, in *Thomas Hardy: The Will and the Way*, Kuala Lumpur

1965, puts forward a highly eccentric (and in my view mistaken) view of Hardy as a kind of Samuel Smiles, who believes that the role of adversity is to offer opportunities that test character, and that the more admirable characters make good use of. This passage is one he lays great stress on, and it is one that does seem to support his argument.

Chapter 4.   *The Social Context*

1 F. E. Hardy, p. 351.

2 This Preface is reprinted in Orel, *Thomas Hardy's Personal Writings,* Kansas 1966, p. 44ff.

3 The sources of this episode, as well as others in the novel, are described by Christine Winfield, in *Nineteenth-Century Fiction* vol. 25 pp. 224–31. This article supplants all earlier speculation on the subject.

4 The fullest treatment is Ruth A. Firor, *Folkways in Thomas Hardy,* NY 1931.

5 Douglas Brown, Thomas Hardy, London 1954, p. 32.

6 The most important of these critics are Arnold Kettle, in his chapter on *Tess* in *An Introduction to the English Novel,* 1953, and in 'Hardy the Novelist': W. D. Thomas Memorial Lecture, Swansea 1966, who claims that the true subject of the novel is the destruction of the English peasantry; Douglas Brown (see Reading List); Raymond Williams (see *Reading List*); and Merryn Williams, *Thomas Hardy and Rural England,* who claims that Hardy succeeds, as no one before him had ever done, in extending the range of English fiction to include a serious treatment of ordinary country folk, and of the rural community at a time of crisis.

7 Merryn Williams, *op. cit.,* p. 91.

8 George Lukacs, *History and Class Consciousness* translated by Rodney Livingstone, London 1971, p. 187.

9 *See* the essay on *The Dorsetshire Labourer.*

10 The arguments are well summarised by J. C. Maxwell (see Reading List).

11 Tönnies, *Community and Association,* translated and supplemented by Charles P. Loomis, London 1955 (especially Book I).

12 *ibid.* p. 64.

13 F. E. Hardy, p. 202.

14 *ibid.* p. 230.

15 Williams, *The City and the Country,* p. 202.

16 The point is well made by John Holloway (see Reading List).

17 Preface to *Selected Poems of William Barnes,* London 1908 (Orel, p. 76).

18 Orel p. 200.

Chapter 5.   *Conclusion*

1 Henry James in *The Nation,* 24 December 1874. See Lerner and Holmstrom, *op. cit.* p. 33.

2 Letter to R. L. Stevenson 19 March 1892, *ibid.,* p. 85.

3 *See,* for instance, Donald Davie, *Thomas Hardy and British Poetry* 1973.

4 Review of *Jude the Obscure* in *Cosmopolis,* January 1896. *See* Lerner and Holmstrom, p. 121.

READING LIST

The most important other novels by Hardy and published by Macmillan are –

Under the Greenwood Tree	1872
Far from the Madding Crowd	1874
The Return of the Native	1878
The Woodlanders	1887
Tess of the D'Urbervilles	1891
Jude the Obscure	1896

Hardy's short pieces are collected in *Thomas Hardy's Personal Writings*, ed. by Harold Orel (University Press, Kansas), 1966 (referred to in the notes as 'Orel'). The most important of these are –

Dialect in Novels	1878
The Dorsetshire Labourer	1883
The Profitable Reading of Fiction	1888
Candour in English Fiction	1890
General Preface to the Novels and Poems	1912

The two volumes of the *Life of Hardy* by his second wife, Florence Emily Hardy, were published in 1928 and 1930; they are now available as a single volume published by Macmillan. As well as the many passages quoted in the text, they include his letter to Rider Haggard on rural England (pp. 312–14).

Contemporary reviews of Hardy's novels (including Gosse's essay on Jude) can be found in either of two collections: Lerner and Holmstrom, *Thomas Hardy and his Readers*, (Bodley Head) 1968, and R. G. Cox, *Thomas Hardy: The Critical Heritage* (Routledge), 1970. The latter is the fuller selection.

There are innumerable books and articles on Hardy, and the following list is highly selective. It includes all those on *The Mayor of Casterbridge* that seem to be of real value, and a shorter selection of good general studies:

Lionel Johnson, *The Art of Thomas Hardy* (London), 1894. The first book on Hardy, and still one of the best, anticipating many critical points that have become quite orthodox.

Lascelles Abercrombie, *Thomas Hardy: A Critical Study* (London), 1912. Another old-fashioned critic. but one who is always sensitive and interesting.

D. H. Lawrence, *Study of Thomas Hardy*, 1932. Available in *Phoenix: Post-humous Papers* (Heinemann). This long essay is well known to all critics of Lawrence, and if only for its notoriety should be mentioned here. Hardy is merely a springboard for Lawrence's tempestuous statement of his own philosophy. He 'rewrites' *Jude the Obscure* as he feels Hardy should have written it, and measures him against a rather grandiose interpretation of Greek tragedy.

A. J. Guerard, *Thomas Hardy* (Prentice Hall), 1949. Sophisticated, intelligent, sometimes controversial.

D. A. Dike, 'A Modern Oedipus: *The Mayor of Casterbridge*', *Essays on Criticism* (1952) Vol. II p. 169ff. Unusual mixture of an archetypal approach, which sees Henchard as the corn god who dies, and a social awareness which discusses the effect of the money economy on Casterbridge life.

Douglas Brown, *Thomas Hardy* (Longmans), London, 1954; and *Thomas Hardy: The Mayor of Casterbridge* (Edward Arnold), 1962. Brown was the first critic to make serious use of the kind of sociological approach I have discussed in Chapter 4. His short book on H. is stimulating but at times unconvincing, and I recommend the monograph on The Mayor in preference.

Julian Moynahan, '*The Mayor of Casterbridge* and the Old Testament's First Book of Samuel', Publications of the Modern Language Association (1956) Vol. LXXI, p. 118ff. Henchard as Saul and Farfrae as David. An unusual and illuminating approach.

John Paterson, '*The Mayor of Casterbridge* as Tragedy', *Victorian Studies* (1959) Vol. III p. 151ff. Overstates the tragic pattern and underrates the realism, but a vigorous, lively discussion that opens many perspectives.

John Holloway, 'H's Major Fiction', *The Chartered Mirror* (Routledge), 1960. Relates the growing pessimism of H's later novels to his vision of the passing of the old rhythmic order of rural England. One of the best of all essays on H.

Robert Heilman, 'H's *Mayor*: Notes on Style', *Nineteenth Century Fiction* (1964) Vol. XVIII, p. 307ff. For consulting rather than reading through. An exhaustive listing and illustrating of H's various stylistic devices, very intelligently done, and full of illuminating insights.

J. C. Maxwell, 'The "Sociological" Approach to *The Mayor of Casterbridge*', *Imagined Worlds*, ed. by Mack and Gregor (London), 1968, p. 225ff. A useful touch of special common sense.

Raymond Williams, *The Country and the City* (Chatto and Windus), 1973, Chapter 18. This is the essay discussed in Chapter 4.